Bitter: The Adversity Principles

The Seven Principles Why God Allows Adversity in a Believer's Life

By David M. Fryson, Esq.

PublishAmerica
Baltimore

© 2003 by David M. Fryson, Esq.

All rights reserved. No part of this book may be reproduced, stored in a retrieval system or transmitted in any form or by any means without the prior written permission of the publishers, except by a reviewer who may quote brief passages in a review to be printed in a newspaper, magazine or journal.

First printing

ISBN: 1-4137-0381-X
PUBLISHED BY PUBLISHAMERICA, LLLP
www.publishamerica.com
Baltimore

Printed in the United States of America

DEDICATION/ACKNOWLEDGMENTS

This book is dedicated to my wonderful family especially to my magnificent and beautiful wife Joy Morris Fryson, who has lovingly taken care of me for the last 27 years. Joy is my partner, my friend, and the love of my life who has dedicated her life to my visions. To my children David Jr., Aaron and Kristina who are each talented in their own right and have the wonderful heart of their mother as well as her breathtaking attractiveness. To my parents, Mrs. Dorothy Fryson and the late Deacon Sim Fryson, my brothers and sisters, Janice Corbett, John Hawkins, Cora Christian, Sim E. Fryson, Jr., Paul V. Fryson and the late Dorothy "Dot" Strawther, but especially to my brother Paul who has been my life's fellow traveler, and my sisters Cora and Janice who have always supported me in ministry.

To my closest friends Pastor Matthew Watts, the late Pastor Robert Patterson and wife Patricia Patterson, Delores Smith, James "Bucky" and Julie Barksdale, Aarin Phillips, Brian Tarr and his late wife Willagene, and William and Pat Hutchens who have been very supportive. Thanks to Sable and Bob Bobier, and Becky and Will Wright who were willing to review my manuscript and make suggestions. Finally, I give a special acknowledgement to the members of the Restoration Community Fellowship Church who are supporting our latest dream of serving Christ through restoration.

Most of all I acknowledge our wonderful Father God who through His Son, our Lord and Savior Jesus Christ, has shown to us His character of love by not only creating us but redeeming us by His Blood. All Glory, Majesty and Honor to Him who is able to keep us from falling through the sweet communion of His Holy Spirit.

Unless otherwise indicated, Bible quotations are taken from the King James Version of the Bible.

TABLE OF CONTENTS

PRINCIPAL I: GOD ALLOWS ADVERSITY FOR THE DEVELOPMENT OF HIS PEOPLE

INTRODUCTION TO THE
ADVERSITY PRINCIPLE ...9

CHAPTER 1
HOW GOD WORKS HIS PERFECT
WILL IN THE CHRISTIAN'S LIFE ...13

PRINCIPAL II: GOD ALLOWS ADVERSITY TO REVEAL THE CHRISTIAN'S UNKNOWN AREAS OF MISTRUST

CHAPTER 2
HOW ADVERSITY REVEALED THE
FEARFULNESS OF JOB ...22

CHAPTER 3
ADVERSITY AND THE CHALLENGE OF FEAR ...35

PRINCIPAL III: GOD ALLOWS ADVERSITY TO PREPARE CHRISTIANS TO BE FIT VESSELS FOR HIS SERVICE

CHAPTER 4
HOW GROWING THROUGH ADVERSITY EMPOWERED
JOSEPH TO BE A LEADER WITHOUT PRIDE
...45

CHAPTER 5
THE PROBLEM WITH PRIDE ...61

PRINCIPLE IV: GOD ALLOWS ADVERSITY TO TEACH CHRISTIANS THE LESSONS OF TRUST

CHAPTER 6
HOW GOD USED ADVERSITY TO HEAL MOSES' LACK OF TRUST CHAPTER ...70

PRINCIPAL V: GOD ALLOWS ADVERSITY TO TEACH CHRISTIANS HIS AGAPE LOVE

CHAPTER 7
ADVERSITY AND MODERN PRESUMPTIONS ...80

CHAPTER 8
DOES THE BIBLE INSTRUCT US TO LOVE OURSELVES? ...88

PRINCIPAL VI: GOD ALLOWS ADVERSITY TO GIVE CHRISTIANS THE PROPER PERSPECTIVE OF THIS WORLD AND THE WORLD TO COME

CHAPTER 9
PAUL AND THE PROSPERITY OF THE GOSPEL ...100

CHAPTER 10
HOW GOD INTENDS TO PROSPER CHRISTIANS ...107

PRINCIPAL VII: GOD ALLOWS ADVERSITY BECAUSE CHRISTIANS ARE SOLDIERS IN A GREAT CONTROVERSY BETWEEN GOOD AND EVIL

CHAPTER 11
HOW THE CHRISTIAN SHOULD
RESPOND TO ADVERSITY ...114

CHAPTER 12
THE CHURCH AND THE ADVERSITY
OF HER MEMBERS ...121

CHAPTER 13
APPLICATIONS OF THE ADVERSITY PRINCIPLES FOR THE LAST DAYS
...128

INTRODUCTION TO THE ADVERSITY PRINCIPLES

PRINCIPLE I: GOD ALLOWS ADVERSITY FOR THE DEVELOPMENT OF HIS PEOPLE

Are you bitter because of the adversity that has entered your life? Have you ever questioned why God would allow you or others to go through trials and difficulty? Do you harbor latent fears that cause you to wonder whether adversity will enter your life and, if so, whether you will be able to withstand its power? More importantly, do you really believe that God has started a great work in you, yet your ability to accept the next level of your calling is obstructed by the alienation that accompanies mistrust? If the answer to any of these questions is yes, an examination of the seven principles of why God permits a believer to experience adversity will be important to your Christian development.

Adversity is the misfortune, calamity and trouble that we find in this world. Mankind's subjection to adversity seems contrary to our vision of God as a loving, merciful Father. Unless we have a proper foundation, it is admittedly difficult to reconcile the paradox of how evil and the resulting pain, suffering and unhappiness can exist in the presence of a loving God.

In the process of our life's journey we all have issues. When we become Christians only one of the issues is immediately settled: the need for salvation. Salvation is the wonderful gift of God, bought by the sacrifice of our Lord and Savior Jesus Christ. The problem is that we continue to live in this environment saddled with the character traits of a lifetime of sin and the generational vestiges of our ancestors' sins. Even though we have these negative character traits, our Heavenly Father is endeavoring to use us to reach others with His Good News of Salvation. In order to prepare us for service God allows us to deal with adverse situations that will help us to grow in the grace He has provided.

Unfortunately, Christians have often done more to disparage the character of God by trying to explain the human dilemma than those who openly oppose the concept of a loving Father. If we have not carefully considered and studied God's position on adversity, we are apt to unwittingly misrepresent why mankind experiences trials, tribulations and tests.

It is imperative that we examine our own presumptions. Many Christians are operating from erroneous presumptions about God. While some operate from the erroneous presumption that it is a virtue to be poor, others go to the other extreme and believe that God wants all of His people to be rich. Many Christians believe that the Bible teaches them to love themselves while others practice self-loathing. We need to examine ourselves to insure that we are truly in the faith with our belief systems.

Some Christians are troubled that adversity is allowed into their lives, even after their commitment to God's service and leading. Many of these believers suppose that since they have accepted God as their Father, through Jesus Christ, they should then be placed in a position where the enemy cannot touch them. Christianity, they reason, should be a kind of free safety zone of peace, comfort and security. When the intensity of Satan's attacks increases rather then decreases, it is easy for this mind-set to lead to bitterness and disillusionment about God's love and care.

People who are disillusioned and bitter use many reasons to justify their negative view of life. I had the privilege to be reared by a person who epitomized the fact that one can have joy despite negative circumstances. My father was one of the most positive and joyful people that I have ever known yet, his life had more than its share of adversity. Through his example I came to my initial understanding that there is really no excuse for bitterness in a Christian's life. The more we go through the more that we can testify of God's goodness, mercy and grace.

Adversity experiences also provide an opportunity for the display of a Christian's faith relationship. When we have joy through adversity we provide a positive testimony for the unsaved to learn of the goodness of God through our example.

This book will consider seven Biblical reasons or principles that operate to allow Christians to encounter adversity. The Seven Principles of Adversity are as follows:

PRINCIPLE I: GOD ALLOWS ADVERSITY FOR THE DEVELOPMENT OF HIS PEOPLE

"All things work together for good to them that love the Lord and are the called according to his purpose." (Romans 8:28)

PRINCIPLE II: GOD ALLOWS ADVERSITY TO REVEAL THE CHRISTIAN'S UNKNOWN AREAS OF MISTRUST

"For the thing which I greatly feared has come upon me, and that which I was afraid of is come unto me." (Job 3:25)

PRINCIPLE III: GOD ALLOWS ADVERSITY TO PREPARE CHRISTIANS TO BE FIT VESSELS FOR HIS SERVICE

"...ye thought evil against me but God meant it unto good, to bring to pass, as it is this day, to save much people alive." (Gen. 50:20)

PRINCIPLE IV: GOD ALLOWS ADVERSITY TO TEACH CHRISTIANS THE LESSONS OF TRUST

"And they overcame him by the blood of the Lamb, and by the word of their testimony; and they loved not their lives unto the death." (Rev. 12:11)

PRINCIPLE V: GOD ALLOWS ADVERSITY TO TEACH CHRISTIANS HIS AGAPE LOVE

"And to know the love of Christ, which passes knowledge, that ye may be filled with all the fullness of God. (Eph 3:19)

PRINCIPLE VI: GOD ALLOWS ADVERSITY TO GIVE CHRISTIANS THE PROPER PERSPECTIVE OF THIS WORLD AND THE WORLD TO COME

"Beloved, think it not strange concerning the fiery trials which Is to try you, as though some strange thing happened unto you." (Peter 4:12)

PRINCIPLE VII: GOD ALLOWS ADVERSITY BECAUSE CHRISTIANS ARE SOLDIERS IN A GREAT CONFLICT BETWEEN GOOD AND EVIL

"And the dragon was wroth with the woman, and went to make war with her seed, which keep the commandments of God, and have the testimony of Jesus Christ." (Rev. 12:17)

The adversity experiences that we encounter as Christians will fit into one of these seven categories. When closely examined, every trial, temptation and test we overcome will reflect the love of God and His care for our lives. The Biblical account of adversity in believers' lives provides us with thrilling examples of how God works His perfect will in the lives of His redeemed.

Prepare yourself to be blessed by adversity.

PRINCIPLE I: GOD ALLOWS ADVERSITY FOR THE DEVELOPMENT OF HIS PEOPLE

CHAPTER 1
HOW GOD WORKS HIS PERFECT WILL IN THE CHRISTIAN'S LIFE

"All things work together for good to them that love the Lord and are the called according to his purpose." Romans 8:28

A young man faced the dilemma of whether God could be trusted for all of the issues of his life. Although he had consulted many counselors, he just could not believe that the God of heaven was concerned about his particular circumstances. He was looking for an answer to the fears that plagued his life. Fear of failure, fear of the future and other fears overwhelmed him as he tried to find meaning in his life. He wondered whether God even heard his prayers and, if He did ever answer them, how would he even know God's voice.

One moonless night, the young man pensively walked through a dark train tunnel onto a highly elevated train track trestle in the tall mountains of West Virginia. He was new to the area and the night was pitch black. Suddenly, out of the darkness, he heard a distant noise. Although he was initially startled, he continued walking on the high level bridge. A few moments later he felt a low rumble and saw the glare of headlights. Only then did he realize that he was in front of a quickly approaching train. Fear gripped him. His mind raced and his feet automatically turned to their highest running gear as the train barreled down on him. After he mindlessly ran for a while, his thoughts cleared and he knew that he only had two choices, continue to run and try to make it to the end of the bridge or... jump.

As the train advanced so close that he could feel the heat of the engine, he acknowledged that it was too far to reach the end of the bridge. At the last possible moment, he did the unthinkable and leaped into the darkness of the night. As he was falling helplessly through the air, he frantically reached out for something solid on which to grasp, but to no avail.

Miraculously, after he had fallen for some time, he was able to grab a protruding support post. Gripping tightly as splinters dug into his hands, the man hung to the post. Suspended in mid air, his legs swung aimlessly. After the train roared past, silence filled the vacuum. Alone and helpless in the dark he dangled precariously.

"Help! ...Oh God, please help me!" he screamed into the stillness. He listened intently. Nothing. In the quiet he held on. His future seemed uncertain as he hung there surrounded by the quiet, pitch-black darkness of a shadow-less night facing the adversity of an unknown future. He again screamed for help and questioned, "Is anybody out there?" After a brief silence the man heard a still small voice that simply said, "Fear not ...just let go." Could it be God? Could God be telling him to jump into the unknown? The man responded quickly, "Is anybody else out there?"

No response, only silence filled the night air. On through the foggy endless night he gripped and hung there. His only hope was to cling ... or was it? That still small voice... should he have heeded the call?

The hours dragged. Gnats flew around his head. Sweat dripped from his forehead and his muscles ached, as pain surged through his shoulders. In the distance, a branch broke the stillness. Still, he clutched the post. Finally, just as his grip weakened and he felt he was about to fall to a certain death, the break of day, with its accompanying soft rays of emergent light, revealed itself over the mountains to begin the dawn of a new day. When the young man's eyes adjusted to the morning light he looked down, only to realize, to his hapless chagrin, the hidden truth: He was only three feet off of the ground.

This story is illustrative of the adversity principles. The young man had trust issues with God that needed to be reconciled. He, like most of us, needed to learn the basic principle of adversity; *God allows adversity into believers' lives for our development.* If we learn to recognize God's voice through the study of His word and prayer and meditation, our lives will be enhanced through our adversity experiences. By yielding to His leading, we will be drawn closer to God's purpose for our lives as we learn to let go. Ultimately, our relationship with the Master will be enhanced because our experiences have taught us that God can be trusted in all of the circumstances of our lives. When all is said and done we will realize that during the times of our adversity experiences we were only three feet off of the ground. Confidence in the Father's care helps prepare us for a life of continuing spiritual growth as we increasingly embrace the lessons of trust learned through adversity.

Through the years mankind has attempted to understand why God would allow difficulty in this life. Theologians have coined the term "Theodicy" for our attempts to understand and explain sin and human suffering in light of asserting that God is good and loving. Our efforts to explain why bad things happen to what seem to be innocent people, will fall far short of revealing the depth of divine justice without the foundation that God Himself provides. Some have postulated that we live in a random universe so random things happen. Others have suggested that since God is in control he is at fault for even the negative things that occur.

While it would a big mistake to come up with pat answers to difficult problems, a review of the Biblical record reveals that trust is the ultimate result of knowing that God can utilize all of the experiences of our lives for His glory. A crucial building block for trust is to see how God has cared for His Children through the ages.

In order to know enough of the answers we need to develop this trust, we must delve deeply into the record that our all-knowing Creator has provided in the Bible. When we have a clearer understanding how God protected His chosen in the Bible, we are better able to understand His care for our lives. One of the primary reasons God allows adversity into a Christian's life is for the development of trust. Adversity Principle Number 1 is simple: *God allows adversity for the development of His people*. God promises us in his word that "all things work together for good to them that love the Lord and are called according to his purpose," (Roman 8:28).

Although we live in a world compromised by the sin issue, Christ supplies current forgiveness and the power to overcome sin. He will also eventually provide an eternal escape from evil, with its resultant pain and suffering. In the meantime, Christians are pilgrim warriors in the front line battle against an evil foe (the devil) who continues to wage war, although the outcome has already been determined against him. The war is real and the casualties are many. To overcome the enemy, we must embrace Christ's lordship of our lives. In fact, we are promised that as we draw near to the risen Christ, we will more closely resemble His character, which will allow us to prevail, through His strength, against the attacks of the enemy. Through it all we have been provided a way of escape from the power of sin as we continue to engage.

In order to have a better understanding of why God allows the redeemed to go through adversity, we need a clear picture of the battle lines that God Himself has drawn. The Bible presents for us an awesome picture of how God is shielding us as we wage this war against Satan and his kingdom. The ultimate Theodicy is found as we discover God's total involvement in every detail of the lives of Biblical characters. God's treatment of the Biblical characters as they dealt with their trials actually reveal for us the answers to the dilemma of why we are allowed to face adversity. We have a perfect defense for our faith and an understanding of why God allows adversity is an important element.

Lets examine in detail the glorious promise of Romans 8:28: "And we know that all things work together for good to them that love God, to them who are the called according to His purpose." This often-quoted text provides a glimpse into how God cares for and delivers His children. This text provides the framework for our Theodicy as we consider how God deals with those who have placed their trust in Him. Unfortunately, many that call upon this text in times of crisis actually have no right to claim its promise.

The promise of the first clause, "[a]ll things work together for good," is reserved in the second clause "to them who love the Lord." How do we know if someone loves the Lord? Christ himself informs us that if we love Him we will keep His Commands (John 14:15). John follows up with the admonition that we are lying if we say we love the Lord and yet do not keep His words (I John 2:4). The question that we must each ask is whether we really love the Lord and, if so, do we show it by the way that we order our life?

We must not use this self-searching text to support our own

sectarian view of God's demand on another Christian's life. We are only accountable for that which we are under knowledge and conviction. Many Christians, who do not currently seem to be reflecting God's best, are still under this enabling provision because they are increasingly walking in the light stream that leads to Godliness. While we are not to judge others, it is crucial to judge ourselves with the understanding that our obedience is evidence of our love. The text is for self-analysis and teaches us that if we live our lives according to God's *revealed will* we are in the position for God to work His *perfect will* in our lives.

The principle of living to the dictates of God's word is often confused with the dangers of legalism. Legalism is when we attempt to secure God's favor and earn salvation by our works. Legalism, at best, is nothing more than an outward compliance to a set of rules (i.e., keeping the law). We are saved by grace through faith in our Savior, Jesus Christ. While God's Law is the living, breathing expression of His will, we are only able to live in God's will by utilizing the power that His grace provides. The same power of grace that saves us also allows us to live Godly lives. This is the discipline of grace and the transforming power of grace enables Christians to live holy and overcoming lives. Unfortunately, the Church has often accepted legalism within its ranks because it causes people to have an outward comportment of conformity. God is looking for those whose outward behavior is a reflection of their inward relationship with Him.

The next provision of Romans 8:28 further narrows the promise to those who are "the called." What does it mean to be "the called"? The "called" are those who are accepting the leading of God in their lives. Christians have heard God's call and have responded by allowing Him to have control. Although we are all on differing levels of submission to God's call, we should all be in the process of giving Christ total control of our lives.

While we often limit the label "the called" to those who have been led to preach in a pulpit ministry, a calling is simply an invitation by God. God has called every Christian to ministry and the answer to the call is found in submission. In fact, the Greek word that the apostle Paul uses for the term "the called" is "Kletos," which means invited or appointed. God calls us by inviting us to be ambassadors for the Kingdom. Christians are appointed to be ambassadors of God that is actuality ministry. While we may not all be called to preach we are all called to submit ourselves as God's ambassador/ministers.

Now that we have identified the class for whom the provisions of Roman 8:28 are for, we can now review the lives of committed Bible characters to see how God worked out this provision in the lives of those who were the most committed to Him. As we review the lives of the giants of faith, we surprisingly find that God often used adversity and trials to solve the innermost problems of their hearts. An understanding of how adversity is used for the development of God's "called" causes us to change our view of the trials we face. As we review their situations, we can see that in all of the circumstances of their lives, including those times of trial and adversity, God was with them and was leading them into the paths of righteousness.

Remember, Romans 8:28 says "*all things* (not some things) work together for good to them who love God and are the called according to His purpose." Christians need a clear knowledge of the Biblical examples of adversity in order to discover how God uses these experiences for the perfecting of His Saints. Actually, we often do not have the proper perspective to fully realize the working of these principles in our own lives during times of trials. As we read the Biblical account of the righteous, we are given a clearer perspective of how God utilizes adversity for the perfection of our character. The Biblical account of what is going on behind the scenes on Earth when God's chosen are experiencing adversity and the occasional glimpses we are given into what is transpiring in the heavenly corridors gives us present hope when we are in the midst of troubles.

The adversity principles in general are important because our calling is according to "His" purpose. This first principle, which informs us that *God allows adversity for the development of His people*, is foundational for all of the other principles. The truth that God allows adversity for our Christian development is particularly important for those whose lives are committed to God's purpose, but through family traits, psychological makeup, intergenerational sins, or other circumstances, have areas of mistrust hidden deep in the recesses of their hearts. These hidden traits are a hindrance because they keep us from the Master's best and obscure us from His great purpose to use us in spectacular ways.

BITTER OR BETTER: THE ADVERSITY PRINCIPLES

Traits such as pride, fear and deceitfulness are issues that lurk deep in the psyche and must be exposed before they can be expunged from the heart of the believer. These conditions are all based upon a lack of trust. The exposure of these hidden issues is crucial in order for believers to experience God's best for ministry as we grow in grace and learn to trust through surrender.

God searches our hearts and knows our innermost areas of need that surfaces as mistrust. As Christ makes intercession for us, he endeavors to root out these unknown areas of mistrust. "And he that searches the hearts knows what is the mind of the Spirit, because he makes intercession for the saints according to the will of God," (Romans 8:27).

As Christ makes intercession for us, he searches our hearts through the indwelling of the Holy Spirit, and identifies our areas of weakness. He then exposes these weaknesses through the allowance of adversity. As we learn the lessons of trust while we go through our adversity experiences we are only then placed in the position to be obedient servants. Genuine obedience is a natural consequence of surrender that manifests itself as trust. A totally surrendered Christian is an obedient servant because all of the issues that lead to disobedience are being exposed and surrendered before the Lord for healing.

God will increasingly be able to use us as all of the sin issues, including the heretofore hidden ones, have been presented for God's forgiving and healing power. Then we will be able to more fully present ourselves as "living sacrifices." Until confronted, these hidden areas of mistrust provide legal ground for the enemy to cause havoc as he tries to provide reasons for Christians to doubt God.

Confusion about God's allowance of trials, tribulations and tests causes many Christians to become bitter when adversity inevitably enters their lives. There are far too many bitter Christians. Whether because of a current crisis, or the vestiges of past adverse experiences, bitterness must be rooted out of our hearts in order for us to properly embrace the fruit of the Spirit. Bitterness keeps us from experiencing the fruit of love, joy, peace, longsuffering, gentleness, goodness, faith, meekness and temperance (See Gal. 5:22). When Christians become bitter because of their adversity experiences, they simply do not understand the principle that God allows Christians to encounter affliction in this sin-tainted environment to make us better. Consider this point in a little more detail.

In a world compromised by the blight of sin, provisions have been made which allow the enemy's attacks to be used for God's glory and for the perfecting of the Saints. Now before you reject the thought of God using the enemy for our good, remember that God is Sovereign and nothing is beyond His ultimate will. Let me assure you, I am in no way suggesting that there is anything good about Satan's motives when he attacks and devises evil against us. There is no praise here for evil or for suffering. However, I do assert, with the confidence that only experience brings, that Satan is confined and restrained by the will of God. What Satan endeavors for evil against us, God uses for our good as we submit to His sovereign will. An important part of the mystery of how God works His perfect will in our lives is revealed when we learn to embrace the sovereignty of God in all of our circumstances.

Satan can prevail against us in these hidden areas that become sanctuaries of doubt, whether known or unknown. This sanctuary of doubt provides legal ground for Satan's spiritual presence in our lives. Our hearts are to be the sanctuary for God's Holy Spirit, but two cannot inhabit the same space. Make sure you get this — God is endeavoring to correct us by rooting out these areas of legal ground that are the areas of Satan's attack.

Satan has legal ground to attack us in the area of our mistrust whether we are aware of the problem or not. Paradoxically, since Satan is allowed to attack in areas where he has legal ground, God is able to use these attacks to help reveal Christian's hidden faults and areas of weakness. Once revealed we have the opportunity to go to God for the forgiveness and healing that will make us whole. The wonderful God we serve is even able to use the attacks of the enemy for our development.

While the adversity principles are more evident when revealing our faults and areas of mistrust, God also can reveal our true gifts during these special times of reckoning. Many times, our true ministry gifts are hidden until trials come to make us utilize them for God's glory. Additionally, the adversity principles can also be used by God to help crystallize our known gifts.

BITTER OR BETTER: THE ADVERSITY PRINCIPLES

How have you handled the adversity that has entered your life? Have you gotten bitter or better with each challenge? We need to consider all of these principles in order to understand more clearly how God teaches us through adversity to serve and love Him without a trace of bitterness. A fresh examination of some of the most well known stories of the Bible will show us how God will be with us through the adverse experiences of our lives. Joseph, Job, Moses and Paul had adverse experiences in their lives that God used to perfect their characters. When we examine the innermost problems of their hearts we can see how God used the difficulties that they encountered to expose their latent problems such as fear, pride, self-sufficiency and even childhood issues that were often hidden deep in the recesses of their hearts. The exposure of these problems through adversity and allowed them to grow in His grace.

We will start with the life of Job. Job's life is an excellent example of how the adversity principles are used by God to prepare us to be fit vessels for His service. Always remember Adversity Principle Number 1, *God allows adversity for the development of His people.*

PRINCIPLE II: GOD ALLOWS ADVERSITY TO REVEAL THE CHRISTIAN'S UNKNOWN AREAS OF MISTRUST

CHAPTER 2
HOW ADVERSITY REVEALED THE FEARFULNESS OF JOB

"For the thing which I greatly feared has come upon me, and that which I was afraid of is come unto me." Job 3: 250

Imagine how your spiritual relationship would be compromised if you were constantly afraid that God was out to get you. Before you answer, you should realize that you might actually be serving the Lord out of a motivation of fear. Whether we admit it or not, many Christians react to God as if He is ready to pounce and destroy our loved ones or us whenever we step out of line. This view of God is more common within the household of faith than you would imagine. Can you conceive of having a strong relationship with God, yet your heart being riddled by fear and trepidation and you not even realize it? Adversity Principle Number 2 informs us that *God allows adversity to reveal the Christian's unknown areas of mistrust.* The Bible provides a surprising example of a person "who loved God" and had been "called according to His purpose" yet had hidden areas of mistrust and sin that needed to be revealed.

The life of Job is one of the most often told stories in the Old Testament. Job's life is usually considered from the perspective of how God allowed Satan to challenge him and his self-righteous response. While that perspective is certainly appropriate, the Biblical account of Job is also an illustration of how God is able to work out problems that we may have in our innermost hearts, as he leads us through the adversity that Satan brings.

This may come as a surprise to some, but much of Job's pre-adversity relationship with God was built on a foundation of fear. In fact, throughout his story we see how God used the dramatic circumstances of Job's life to bring him into a more trusting relationship. Before his adversity experience, Job was afraid for his own experience, he was afraid for the experience of his children, and most importantly, his fears were causing him to worship God inappropriately. Job's story is a compelling example to consider because God has provided a unique behind the curtain view of a heavenly experience.

The scene opens as we view a heavenly council when the "sons of God came to present themselves before the LORD" (See Job 1:6-12). While we do not have the information to know what beings were actually present at this meeting, it is thrilling to contemplate that the Creator would have convened a meeting where His living creation would come to present themselves before Him. Can you imagine the splendor and majesty of this great celestial gathering? This may have been a situation where all of the created beings were gathered or one where a representative council was convened.

Satan then made his accusations against Job. He accused Job of only serving God because of the hedge of protection the Lord had put around him. This was a continuation of the criticism of God that Satan had begun in heaven before his expulsion. The evidence suggests that Satan's rebellion in heaven included accusations brought by the evil one that accused God of being a tyrant. Satan had insinuated that the only reason that creatures served the Creator was out of self-motivations such as fear or to have the protection and provisions that God makes for His children. This was an attack on the foundation of God's Kingdom and was a direct denunciation of God's ability to inspire loyalty purely out of love and devotion. Satan's suggestion that Job served God for any other reason other than love was also a criticism of the unfallen beings who, unlike Satan and the 1/3 of the angels who committed to him, remained loyal to the Creator.

One might wonder why Satan, the accuser of the brethren, was even at this heavenly council since he had earlier been forcibly removed from the presence of God. It is possible that Satan was at this celestial gathering because father Adam had given his scepter of dominion of the Earth over to the adversary through his fall in the Garden of Eden. You will remember that Satan's rebellion against God started in heaven while he was still known as Lucifer. When Lucifer, through pride, had exhausted the limit of God's mercy, there was war in heaven and Michael and his angels fought and prevailed against Satan and his angels. Satan fell like lightening to the earth (See Rev. 12:7; Lk. 10:18).

If so, imagine in this representative counsel the other representatives were there to present themselves and represent their constituencies. Satan, as mankind's representative who was there because of Adam's sin, did not represent his constituency, but was there to accuse the best that the race had to offer. Thank God that our Savior, Jesus Christ, has wrested the scepter from the hand of the enemy. We need a Savior to represent us, not an adversary.

God then asked Satan where had he been, and more importantly what had he been up to. It was not that God did not know where Satan had been or what devious activities he had been carrying out. I believe that the question was asked to reestablish in Satan and for us as observers, that the evil one was still accountable to Him who is the Creator and Sustainer of all life.

Satan responded that he had been going "to and fro on the earth." Later revelation informs us that we should be sober and vigilant because this same Satan "as a roaring lion walks about, seeking whom he may devour,"(I Pet. 5:8). On this occasion, Satan was seeking to devour Job as he endeavors to devour us on a daily basis.

Under this framework of contention, the Father allowed Satan to confront Job with the adversity of losing all that was precious to him, his wealth, his community standing and, most importantly, his children. After Job survived his first loss without cursing God, Satan requested permission to intensify his trial by attacking Job's health. The second request was also granted but Satan was precluded from taking Job's life. As soon as he had the permission and opportunity, Satan inflicted as much pain and suffering as possible by covering Job's body with painful sores from the soles of his feet to the crown of his head (See Job 2:1-10). Throughout all of his adversity Job remained steadfast and did not curse God.

As we view Job's situation, we are given a unique behind-the-scene insight into how God was always in control of the area of Satan's attack and the intensity thereof. It is imperative to understand that in all that happens to us as Christians, God is always in ultimate control and, because He is Sovereign, we can always trust Him for the outcome. While Satan's attacks were possible because Job had some areas in his life that needed the growth that adversity can bring, he was never outside of the protection and providence of the Master.

Job's religious experience needed to grow. Although he was said to be perfect and upright, Job's "perfection" was in that he lived and allowed his life to be ordered within the truth that he knew. However, this "perfection" did not exempt Job from the need to develop in his relationship with God, and his story bears this out. Let's consider the downside of Job's religious experience before his adversity experience.

What we often view as Job's diligence is nothing more than an illustration of how his relationship with God needed to be deepened. For instance, when Job rose up early and offered burnt offerings for his children, he was "afraid" that his children might sin by cursing or renouncing God (Job 1:4). Before we applaud Job for his diligence there were at least two problems with this sacrifice.

First, there is no Biblical authority for sacrificing for sins not yet committed. It was presumptuous for Job to offer a prospective sin offering for his children and it was indicative of his fear. Job was so afraid that he or his children would suffer from the wrath of God that he failed to trust Him. In other words, Job's fear was causing him to worship God in an inappropriate manner.

You see, unlike the heathen perspective of sacrifice, the sacrificial service system was not given to appease an angry and vengeful God, who had to be held at bay because he would pounce and destroy at the first hint of mistake. A thousand times No! The sacrificial system pointed to the sacrifice that our loving God would make on our behalf through His Son, Christ Jesus, and to show the depth of His love. While a part of the system was given in order to illustrate that the result of disobedience is death, every component and symbol of the sacrificial system was designed to point to the coming redeemer who would take away the sins of the world. For instance, when a spotless, innocent lamb was slain, it was indicative of how the sinless Savior would be slain for our sin and iniquity.

Job's sacrifices for his children were made inappropriately and out of a motivation of fear. This erroneous perspective Job had about God is important for us to consider because we worship a God who loves and cares for us rather than one who is looking to destroy us because of our sin. When we serve God out of fear, Satan exults that his misrepresentations of the Father are being accepted within the intimacies of human worship. Realizing Job's need for growth in this area of his experience, God allowed him to face a situation that forced him to confront his trust issues.

While Job was afraid for his children's welfare, he should have trusted God for their relationship while praising the Lord for their care. Our Father never wants us to be afraid of Him, fear the future, or fear how he will treat others.

Further, the attempted prophylactic sacrifice of Job was an offense to Him that is "able to keep us from falling." The aim of the sacrificial system was to show that our Heavenly Father, through His love, has provided a way of escape from the penalty of sin. It is through our personal relationship with God, through Jesus Christ, that we are empowered to live uplifted and holy lives not in order to be saved, but because we are saved through the blood of Christ. We are to trust that God will keep us when we commit our lives to him. Listen to the comfort God gives us:

> "Whoever shall confess that Jesus is the Son of God, God dwells in him, and he in God. And we have known and believed the love that God hath to us. God is love, and he that dwells in love dwells in God, and God in him. Herein is our love made perfect, that *we may have boldness in the day of judgment* because as he is, so are we in this world. *There is no fear in love; but perfect love cast out fear because fear hath torment. He that fears is not made perfect in love.*"
> (I John 4:15-18 (italics added for emphasis))

Fear is a tormenting factor in our lives. One commentator has suggested that there are more than 300 scriptural references of God telling His people to not be afraid. Fear is so tormenting, that God gives us a "do not be afraid" for virtually every day in the year. Job's lack of trust was causing him to be fearful even in his approach to worship and sacrifice and he needed to learn that He who created existence could be trusted for our existence. We too must learn to trust God for all of the circumstances of our lives. It is not until we realize that the sacrifice of Christ allows us to have "boldness in the Day of Judgment" that we then will be able to truly celebrate the love of Christ in our hearts.

I cannot imagine that Job's worship was celebratory in nature before his encounter with adversity. Since he was being controlled by fear, he had precious little to celebrate. The discussion on worship styles often centers on whether the church service should be solemn or upbeat and celebratory. There is often a wide gap between the adherents of these worship styles. Many fear the day of judgment of God and their relationship with Christ is controlled by the fear that their name may come up for examination at any time. Contrary to being fearful, the scriptures assures us that when we are in Christ's love we can have assurance or boldness in the Day of Judgment.

All of the discussion in the world cannot convince someone to celebrate when his or her relationship with God is fostered on self. This type of relationship manifests itself in trying to be acceptable by what we can do rather than centering on whom we belong. When we come to the realization of the great things God has done for us our worship will automatically be a celebration. We will celebrate, not in order to have a good time, but as a natural outgrowth of recognizing what God has done. Realizing God's goodness introduces us to the wonders of celebrating His presence. When we are in the presence of God and realize what He has done for us we can't help but celebrate His goodness, His mercy and His awesome grace. Just thinking about it makes me want to shout.

The second problem with Job's attempted intercession for his children concerned the burnt offering that he offered for his children. The burnt offering was to be offered of a person's "own voluntary will"(See Lev.1:3). Job's sacrifice was actually a prayer of selfishness disguised as intercession. Job had developed a "me and mine" relationship with God. The sacrificial system that was designed for personal sin confession was now being used by Job to cover the sins of his children, possibly fearing that they would fail to do so for themselves and he would be faced with their tragedy. Job actually tried to worship on their behalf. We cannot worship for anyone else. What we can do is provide intercession for others. There is an important difference.

While Job's sacrifice had the appearance of being an intercession, it was really a plea that he would not be faced with something happening to his peace through his children's problems. An intercession is using our relationship with God to intercede or "stand in the gap" for someone else. Intercession is when we take our relationship with God almost as surety on behalf of others.

By trying to worship for them, Job's fears for himself were being inappropriately presented under the guise of intercession for others. When we intercede for others, it should be totally selfless. Any intercession that is perverted to selfishness is not pleasing to God and is an indication of a heart that is deceitful. We are, in effect, illustrating that we have not fully comprehended how we are to operate in a kingdom founded on love and selflessness.

God's best for us occurs when our petitions emanate from the root of honesty. We limit the effectiveness of our prayers when our petitions are deceitful, whether knowingly or unwittingly. God can see through our faults and hear us nevertheless. But our Heavenly Father desires his children to be totally honest as we seek His perfect will. God aims to go to the root of our problems because "bitter roots produce bitter fruits."

We can only speculate as to why Job had a heart that was filled with fear. Sometimes, even in Christian households, our approach to God engenders a wrong perspective of God. As children we receive our perspective of what God is like by how our parents or significant caregivers view God and how they treat us. If our parents or caregivers are cruel and unloving, or if they harbor an unrighteous fear of God, these traits are passed to the children's perspective of God. Because of this foundation developed in the home of origin, many Christians develop a toxic faith where God is not viewed and known as our loving Father.

Interestingly, Satan attempts to portray God as stern and rebuking rather than the only One that is ever mindful of what is best for us. It is the misrepresentation of God's character that establishes this type of foundational fear in many believers' hearts and Satan is always pleased to misrepresent God's loving character. One of Satan's favorite methods to obscure the love of God in our experience is by causing us to be afraid. The counterfeit of Satan's fear for God's loving embrace should always be contrasted.

For instance, before the transgression of Adam and Eve in the Garden of Eden, they had no fear. As long as they were in right relationship with the Creator they were fearless in every way. However, once they had knowledge of sin, through the misrepresentation of God's character by Satan, they found themselves out of proper relationship with the Creator, and it caused them to be afraid. After their sin, fear obscured the reality that the Father still loved them and had a plan for their reconciliation.

Importantly, while under the influence of God before their transgression they had no fear of Satan. Tragically, as soon as they gave Satan entrance into their lives they had an unrighteousness "fear" of God.

Remember when God looked for them after their transgression? They tried to hide because they were afraid. Satan knows that as long as we give him place and allow ourselves to be under his domination, we will fear and hide from our Creator. We cannot be motivated and directed by fear and trust at the same time. We must choose one or the other. This does not mean that we will never feel afraid but that we will work through the fear rather than operating within a fearful parameter. We should never allow fear to be our motivation. When we are motivated and controlled by fear, we will react to situations in ways that are not indicative of God's best for our experience.

Importantly, we can feel fear, and not be motivated by it. The fact that we *feel* afraid should not progress into allowing ourselves to be *motivated* and/or controlled by the feeling of fear. The fact that God has instructed us so often to not be afraid is an indication that Christians are subject to feel the emotion of fear. What God is really saying when he tells us to not be afraid is that we must not allow the feeling or emotion of fear to control us.

When we feel fear we should be honest about the emotion as we work through it. Rather then to suppress the fear in denial, we should weigh the fear against God's promises and choose the promise of peace. The fact that Satan pushes the fear button and yet we are still able to operate in trust regardless of the emotion is a testament to God's presence in our lives and is a very strong reproach to the enemy.

After adversity befell him, Job revealed the fear that had captured his heart *before* the tragic circumstances. In Job 3:25 he says, "the thing which I greatly feared is come upon me, and that which I was afraid of is come unto me." Do you get it? Before Job's adversity, he was afraid that the very thing that happened to him would occur.

This is an area of faith that we should not ignore. When we fear something, we are apt to talk our fears. When we talk our fears, the fears become a self-fulfilling prophecy since "death and life are in the power of the tongue" (Prov. 18:21). We must learn to confess our fears but live in trust. While it is permissible to confess our fears to God, we should immediately let go of the fear just as we let go of any potential limitation. Our job is to look for the good and affirm God's goodness, mercy and grace. "Let no unwholesome word proceed from your mouth, but only such a word as is good for edification according to the need of the moment, that it may give grace to those who hear" (Eph. 4: 29).

This admonition from God informs us to always control our conversations, but particularly when we are in the middle of problems and cares. We are to speak according to the "need of the moment." When we speak, it should be in order "that it may give grace to those who hear." This is a wonderful, positive application of the power of our speech.

To confess our fear does not mean to repeatedly talk our fears. We reveal our fears in honesty but then we should immediately express our understanding of the Master's love and devotion to us as well as His promise to keep us in His care. When we are going through adversity one of the most important things to remember is that the greatest weapon in our arsenal of fear resistance is submission to God. The level of our submission to God is directly related to our level of trust. "Submit yourselves therefore to God. Resist the devil and he will flee" (James 4:7). When we submit ourselves to God in trust, Satan loses his power over us. In fact, the enemy runs when we exercise our trust in the awesome power of our God because that coward knows he will be defeated every time. Always talk about your trust in God rather than any possible negative thing that may befall you. *Again, talk trust not fear.*

As we talk our trust rather than our fears Adversity Principle Number 2 becomes manifest in our life. Remember that *God allows adversity to reveal the Christian's unknown areas of mistrust.* Did God want Job to be in fear that bad things would come into his life? Even more importantly, does God want us to live in apprehension that tragedy will befall us, or that we will lose what we have? Should we in any way fear what the future holds for us? To all of these questions the answer is an absolute <u>NO!</u> God forbid! But like Job we must learn to trust God by living through and growing better by our adversity experiences. Part of the solution to how we can overcome is to always have a testimony of trust.

Job had the most brutal things imaginable happen to him. He lost his health, his wealth, his standing in the community and his children. By his own admission that which he feared the most occurred and Job not only lived through it, his relationship with God was deepened as he learned to talk and live in trust. In fact, through it all, the quality of Job's life improved, not just from the externals that were later reestablished to him, but more importantly, from the internal issues of his heart.

What was the quality of Job's life before he learned to trust? Apparently very shaky! Job said that he was not in safety, and had no rest or quiet (Job 3:26). It is a difficult life to have an ongoing "religious" relationship with God, but not know how to trust Him as our loving, caring Father. To know God and his demands on our lives, without understanding that we can trust Him to supply our needs, leads us into a miserable experience.

Many within the Christian world know about God but spend their experience dealing with the issues of obedience rather than living in a trusting relationship that will lead to obedience. It is through adversity that we learn the important lessons of trust. Through trusting God, our relationship with Him becomes real, and when we are real with God our obedience is a natural outgrowth of the relationship. Oh, that we would understand that we can only have true joy in our lives when we have trust through surrender.

Sometimes God must remove that which we are afraid of losing before we can learn to trust Him for those very things. It was not until Job lost his health and wealth, his standing in the community and, most importantly, his children that he learned to trust God for those very things. Later, when all of those things were returned, Job could live life secure in knowing that he could trust God and accept his blessings without fear of loss.

It is beyond the scope of this chapter to fully consider how God was just in His relationship with each of Job's children who lost their lives. One may wonder whether it was just for God to allow Job's children to die in order to deal with the issues of Job's life. While we are not given the particulars about the lives of Job's children, we must rest assured that God was as just and righteous in His dealings with them as He was with Job. God is not out to allow your children to be killed in order to prove a point to you. Yet in the most difficult experiences of our lives, God will develop, comfort and sustain us. Job's lesson was one of trust and that is what we are shown in the examination of this aspect of his life.

The same Job who had feared for his substance and family, now, in the throes of adversity, learned to say with power, "though He slay me yet will I trust him" (Job 13:15). Although God was not trying to kill him, we can see how Job was learning the lesson of trust. In the midst of his adversity, Job's relationship was becoming better as he showed God that he would not become bitter. As he continued to learn to trust God, Job was later to add that no matter what the circumstances, even if it ended in death, he could trust God. We see Job's spiritual maturity increasing when he says "I know that my redeemer lives and that he shall stand at that latter day upon the earth and though after my skin worms destroy this body yet in my flesh I shall see God . . . and I shall see Him for myself... " (See Job 19:25-27).

Job learned that even if he lost everything, including his life, he could have peace when he trusted because God's transcendence would make it possible for him to rise again in the resurrection. Hallelujah... what a promise of learning to trust. After seeming to lose it all, Job found the assurance of knowing that even when the worst of our vain imaginations occurs, God is with us and can still be trusted. Understanding God's transcendence assures us that the sometime terrible present is just a temporary stage that will allow God to show us off as his children. Rather than becoming bitter and cursing God as his wife suggested, Job became better by learning to open his heart to a new level of trusting relationship with the Father.

It is a recurring theme that the God of heaven is endeavoring to bring us into a loving, trusting relationship with Him as we surrender to His Sovereign will. Only when we learn to trust God through total surrender can we fully appreciate His leading in our lives. God is interested in showing the entire universe in general and Satan in particular, that he has people in this sin sick world that trust and love Him. Remember, it was God who asked Satan during the celestial counsel, "Have you considered my servant Job?" God wanted to show off his faithful servant, and Job was up to the task. Are you ready to be used of God? Then learn from the adversity that God allows to come your way and look up, for your redemption draws near.

Finally, we see in Job 42:10, that the "LORD turned the captivity of Job when he prayed for his friends." Job's prayers turned outward after he dealt with the ordeal, and this was another sign of his maturity in trusting God. As long as we harbor a heart full of fear, we will not be able to share the true love of God to others because we will have the focus on self. Job didn't need self-love. He needed to know that God could be trusted. When Job's heart was no longer captive to his fears he was able to be evangelistic because he trusted God for his own situation and could therefore truly intercede on behalf of others. God endeavors to put us in the position to deal with our inner heart issues through the development of our trust so we can ultimately help others.

While we are given the opportunity to see what was occurring behind the scenes, Job, at the time, did not know and was constrained by his situation into a position of trust. There continues to be much that occurs in our lives where God's actual purpose is hidden from our view. Because of those things that are occurring behind the veil of our understanding we, like Job, must learn to have total faith in God's care.

God's plan to utilize us for His glory is limited only by our lack of trust and surrender. Surrender is crucial to our availability as fit vessels for the Master's service. As we submit, every issue of our lives will be made available for God's healing power. Job's fear was limiting his ability to be used of God and the Master did something about it.

The devastating effect of fear should not be underestimated. While God is more than able to meet the challenge of fear in our live we, like Job, must submit ourselves for the healing in order to overcome the grasp of fear. The wonderful message of Adversity Principle Number 2 is that *God allows adversity to reveal our unknown areas of mistrust.* Once revealed and confessed, God will heal and our relationship with the Lord will be made better. God does not cause our adversity but nothing happens to the Christian that has not been weighed by the Master and found that it can be turned to our good as it reveals our areas of mistrust.

CHAPTER 3
ADVERSITY AND THE CHALLENGE OF FEAR

"There is no fear in love; but perfect love cast out fear: because fear hast torment. He that feareth is not made perfect in love." I John 4:18

"But the fearful, and unbelieving, and the abominable, and murderers, and whoremongers, and sorcerers, and idolaters, and all liars shall have their part in the lake which burneth with fire and brimstone: which is the second death." Revelations 21:8

In the Biblical depiction of those who will find themselves outside of God's kingdom and subjected to the second, eternal death, the first group mentioned is those who are "fearful." Revelation 21:8 places the fearful in the same class as the unbeliever, the abominable and the murderer. Why would God place the fearful in the same class as the sexually impure, sorcerers, idolaters and liars? This is a compelling question.

Fear and mistrust is the underlying root for much of our embrace and acceptance of sin. We must surrender all areas of mistrust as we grow in grace. Many times we do not even understand the root of our own fears. That is why Adversity Principle Number 2 is so vitally important: *God allows adversity to reveal the Christian's unknown areas of mistrust.*

While we are often admonished to fear God, the Hebrew word for fear used in these Old Testament admonitions is "yir'ah" which means reverence. Even though God's people are to have an awestruck reverence for Him and His work that the Bible describes as "fear," God does not want his children to be afraid of Him or harbor any apprehension of the future.

Granted, fear is an emotion that has its legitimate place. Fear is the general term to describe the anxiety and agitation felt at the presence of danger. It is appropriate to experience the type of fear that is an immediate and natural defense to danger. Courage is not the absence of fear but the overcoming of its power. If you will remember our opening story, the young man was fearful as he hung on the suspended post but he was instructed not to fear but to just "let go." To hang suspended in the air is an understandably fearful experience. However, to refuse to follow the command of God because of fear is not acceptable.

John informs us, "he that is fearful has not been made perfect in love" (I John 4:18). The type of inappropriate fear that John is referring to is that trepidation which produces a life of anxiety and keeps us from following the leading of God. Fear and anxiety prevents us from resting in the assurance that God can be trusted. When the Christian is fearful, it is evidence of a heart that has not been completely touched by the love of God through Jesus Christ. God exposes the fear hidden deep in our hearts by forcing us to face our deepest anxieties when adversity comes our way. While Satan attempts to destroy us in our points of weakness, God uses the attacks of the enemy to reveal and heal those weaknesses as we are taught trust through surrender.

Interestingly, this inappropriate fear resides in the human heart for various reasons. Many are fearful because they don't understand how to trust that God is in ultimate control of all of the circumstances of their lives. Many others are fearful because they sense an obligation to secure their own destiny. If we are not intimate with the One who holds the future, it is only logical to focus our attention on our own needs. This focus on our own needs will result in anxiety.

Some fear because they have hidden conditions and they dread future exposure. The yoke of disobedience lurks in the deep recesses of their heart and they feel uneasy, fearing exposure at any time. If others don't know about their hidden sins, they reason, maybe God will forget. Yet in their hearts they are never at ease because this inward fear is keeping them from God's best. Still others, because of issues created during their foundational years, or other factors, have a physiological profile that predisposes them to fear issues such as panic attacks and other anxiety and mood disorders.

Fear keeps us from God's best and the fearful heart must be exposed in order to open us to the forgiveness and healing power of Christ Jesus. Satan and his demons have paralyzed the world through fear. The agents of darkness particularly love to terrorize the Church with this malady. They know that fear keeps us from God's best.

The Church has often failed to recognize the inner dimension of fear and the resultant effect. Unfortunately, the Church's response to those who are fearful has often been to castigate those who show external fear while providing no comfort or way out of the dilemma. This causes many Christians to be reluctant to share their trials, which allows fear to fester and expand.

Fear can only be conquered by exposure and will diminish as we expose ourselves to God and our fellow believers. When the Church matures to the point of understanding its role in this healing process, we can be secure in sharing our deepest anxieties within the household of faith.

Conversely, many very successful people owe much of their material success to internal fear. Some of the hardest working people in society in general, and specifically within the body of Christ, work out of a motivation of fear. They relinquish the peace that is the result of an honest relationship with the Prince of Peace and instead attempt to find peace by trying to take care of themselves.

An honest assessment of many that are labeled "workaholic" would reveal that the true motivation behind their work addition is fear. Often those who experienced deprivation in their childhood are afraid of ever being in that situation again. Their lives become unbalanced as they vow to never again suffer lack. The problem with a vow of this kind is that it does not include God in the equation. It is a perverse form of works that says, "God, I believe in you but I must take care of taking care of myself."

The fear that motivates this type of hard work actually brings a type of temporal success. The world is impressed with the work ethic that leads to the material success of these individuals. What is not so apparent is the ultimate futility and miserable conditions of the underlying lifestyle. It is this type of person who ends up falling apart when their success is challenged or their lifestyle in any way declines. They, in effect, have never dealt with the fear issue and it ultimately destroys them.

Christians, including many who are involved in ministry, often cover their fears with a spiritual facade. We talk and preach a fearless stance, yet in our innermost hearts we are covering our fearful condition with outward spiritual bravado. It's time for the people of God to be blatantly honest with themselves and with God so that we may have the open and honest relationship that the Bible projects for the household of faith.

God endeavors to bring us to a close relationship with Him which will ultimately dispel all fear but, in the interim, we must often live through fear while not allowing it to control us. We can have the ultimate joy and peace of knowing that we can trust God regardless of the situation and that He will provide for our needs. Christ was so emphatic in His command to "take no thought" when it comes to our material needs because it shows what master we serve.

> No man can serve two masters: for either he will hate the one, and love the other; or else he will hold to the one, and despise the other. Ye cannot serve God and mammon. Therefore, I say unto you, take no thought for your life, what ye shall eat, or what ye shall drink; nor yet for your body, what ye shall put on. Is not the life more than meat, and the body than raiment? Behold the fowls of the air: for they sow not, neither do they reap, nor gather into barns; yet your heavenly Father feedeth them. Are ye not much better than they? Which of you by taking thought can add one cubit unto his stature? And why take ye thought for raiment? Consider the lilies of the field, how they grow; they toil not, neither do they spin. And yet I say unto you, that even Solomon in all his glory was not arrayed like one of these. Wherefore, if God so cloth the grass of the field, which today is and tomorrow is cast into the oven, shall he not much more clothe you, O ye of little faith.
>
> Therefore take no thought, saying, what shall we eat: or what shall we drink? or wherewithal shall we be clothed?
>
> (For after all these things do the Gentiles seek:) for your Father knoweth that ye have need of all these things. But seek ye first the kingdom of God and His righteousness; and all these things shall be added unto you. Take no thought for the morrow; for the morrow shall take thought for the things of itself. Sufficient unto the day is the evil thereof.
> (Matt.6:25-34)

Christ informs us that we are to take no thought for the things of this life. Unfortunately, most of us spend virtually our entire lives worrying over these things. The message that we must internalize is that we should not worry. Worry is non-productive. We should work and plan, but take no thought in worry that we will not have the things necessary for life. When we take thought for these things, it is an indication that we have not worked through our fear issues.

Our lives will be freed only as we realize that tomorrow is in God's hand and that we should live in the moment. If we allow ourselves to be restricted by our past or put our focus on the provisions needed for tomorrow, it keeps us from receiving the gift of being in the <u>NOW</u>. The present is where God's power is best manifested. When we are focused in the moment, we can be fearless as we watch God provide for our immediate need. In fact, eternity is actually present in the moment. Here's why.

With God there is no past or future, for He is in the ever present. He who created time stands outside of its boundaries. God is not bound by time relationships. Since God is not bound by time, he can be with each of us in a way that is not quite comprehensible to us who have been created in and operate within time's limitations. The reason God has "time" for each of us in a world of five billion people is that He stands beyond the realm of time limitation. God has "time" just for me because He is not limited or bound by it. What a mighty God we serve.

God's ever presence is also a partial explanation why we can be covered for past sins by being in a present relationship with God. While it is not totally within our comprehension, the Bible informs us that when we as Christians "fall away, to renew again to repentance seeing they (we) crucify the Son of God afresh and put Him to an open shame" (Heb.6:6). How can we crucify Christ through our present sin, when He hung on a cross 2,000 years ago? It is enough to boggle the imagination.

God's ever presence is why we have assurance for our provision. He who never slumbers or sleeps is not caught by surprise with tomorrow's circumstances. Don't worry about tomorrow, its in God's almighty hand.

An examination of our fears will reveal that they are usually either rooted in events of the past or apprehension for the future. For instance, some Christians are never able to feel that they have truly been forgiven for past sins. They live their lives rooted in the past. It is easy to be controlled by the bitterness we feel from the abuse encountered in our childhood or other negative events of the past. As long as our lives are controlled by the past, we will not be free to be the person that God intends for us to be now. What we consider to be the dark present is often only that way because of clouds from the past. It is a tragedy to allow past negative experiences to keep us from the bright today that God provides.

Far too many Christians are miserable in their everyday lives because they have failed to resolve issues from the past. When we come to Christ in confession of our sins we are forgiven. No matter how heinous the sin may have been, God gives us total forgiveness. When we completely give the Lord our past He leads us to a brighter tomorrow.

Abuse and other problems encountered in childhood must be revealed and presented for God's healing power. As long as we stay hidden about our problems, Satan uses these secrets to limit the joy of our relationship with God and with others. An environment is needed where Christians can confess their sins to God but their faults to one another. I truly believe that the healing of the experience comes from the telling of the story. The hidden portions of our life are actually areas that we have not confessed and surrendered. Satan attacks us in these not-yet-surrendered areas. In fact, he has legal ground to prevail against us in the areas that we have not surrendered to God.

If you have situations or events from the past that plague you, it is an indication that you have not totally surrendered the pain to God. If your past is limiting you, or if you just cannot seem to overcome depression or sadness, or have a general feeling of unhappiness, I urge you to immediately submit these events through prayer and appropriate Christian counseling. While I believe that the local Church was designed to counsel its members, until such time as the Church is equipped to do so, we should submit ourselves to professional Christian counseling. I assure you that it is worth the effort. We are to live lives that are filled with a complete joy that is not shadowed by our past pain. Anything less is living below our privilege.

While many Christians are limited by their past, a surprising number of Christians are fearful of what tomorrow brings. The fear of the future is a trust issue. Consider how many Christians are actually afraid of the events that will occur just before Jesus returns for His Church. We must be secure in the knowledge that the awesome events to occur on the earth immediately preceding Christ's second return, will actually be a vindication for God's people. We should be looking up for our redemption draws close.

Fear of the impending last day crisis must be reserved for those who do not have a relationship with the Master. The fear of many Christians was recently revealed when the Y2K hoax came on the scene. Many Christians were worried about what would happen when the year 2000 supposedly would overwhelm their computer. Whole ministries devoted their time to sounding this false alarm of the beginning of troubles. Interestingly, when the year 2000 came and nothing negative occurred, very few of these ministries repented for these false prophecies.

Hopefully, the body of Christ will learn that when our minds are focused on the Lord we will shine in the midst of worldly trouble. We should never fear the future. Tomorrow, like yesterday, is in the hand of our Almighty God, who lives in the ever present.

We will rise from a low-energy, fear-based relationship into a high-energy, peace-based union as our minds are increasingly focused on Christ in the moment. We are promised that we will be kept in "perfect peace" when our minds are focused on the Lord. But who among us can honestly say that our minds are stayed on the Lord? This focus is particularly difficult when we are caught up in the things of this world. If our minds are on lands, houses, cars and bank accounts, our minds are not "stayed on the Lord" and we are not focusing where Christ's gift is located, in the present. It may seem trite, but the *gift* is the *present*, and the *present* is a *gift* from God that we should cherish.

Our focus on the present should not be used as an excuse to keep us from the stewardship obligation that God has given to us. We are to be good stewards of all that God has provided, which means that we will take care of those things that He has provided and plan appropriately. The point here is that God will take care of all of our needs so that we have nothing to fear.

The fear issue is a very personal one for me. Due to certain circumstances in my background I, for a substantial period of my life, suffered from what was diagnosed as an anxiety or panic disorder. Although I have been able to function, for the most part, with a high level of energy and achievement, the condition prevented me from achieving God's best for my life. I have lived a blessed life, but the condition was keeping me from the total heartfelt joy that has been promised to the child of God.

For instance, I used to experience the most devastating fear for no apparent reason. My first panic attack occurred when I was only twelve years old when I thought I was just going to die for no reason. The Christian household in which I was reared provided no answers to my situation except for the occasional ridicule, and I learned to keep my fears undercover. Can you imagine that my treating physician prescribed a sedative to me as a 12-year-old child. Even at this young age I knew something was wrong with that and refused to continue on this medication while I worked through the situation alone. I lived with this condition for many years, even after I came to an adult relationship with the Lord.

As I grew in grace, the duality of having a relationship with God yet finding myself being fearful became increasingly difficult. While I witnessed to others about the need to trust in God, my own peace was challenged over situations that most people accomplished without a second thought. There are times when I would present a talk or sermon on peace and then been almost unable to drive home due to anxiety. While my relationship with God was real, fear was keeping me from God's best.

The more hidden I was about my situation the worse it seemed to get. My breakthrough came when I submitted myself to a Christian counseling center that dealt with a holistic approach to dealing with issues of the inner heart. I sought this treatment because I felt God's leading to be removed from the anti-anxiety medication that had been prescribed to deal with the symptoms of this disorder. Importantly, my healing was not instantaneous. I have been gradually changed by the power of God.

Imagine, being afraid of heights and growing up in the mountains of West Virginia. At one time fear and anxiety kept me from doing such mundane tasks as crossing a bridge (Charleston, WV is a river city). Just being in a "high place" would cause me to experience an almost paralyzing fear. While I still suffer some residual uncomfortable feelings with heights, I have been healed from this malady. Although dealing with this disorder has been difficult throughout my life, I consider myself a blessed man.

Through the adversity of this condition, I have been placed in a situation of daily dependence. I have seen through my personal experience and healing how God has used this adversity, this thorn in the flesh, to keep me humble and dependent on Him. I have also seen the rewards of being put in the position of daily trust.

Many have commented on what seems to be my calm in the midst of trouble, and my fearless stance on public issues. When I reveal that I have suffered with this condition most people are completely surprised. God continually puts me in positions to stand when others fear. It is only through the trust that I have gained through the adversity of my disorder that God has been able to use me to stand in some very unusual situations.

I know from this personal experience that God will use us in the very point of our perceived weakness rather than our perceived strength. I thank the Lord for His healing power and I give Him the glory, realizing that He can be trusted for all the issues of our lives. By overcoming, through God's grace, this adverse life experience, I can testify that God continues to work with and through me for His glory.

My experience is an example of how God uses us in our point of weakness. In fact, when the Apostle Paul was dealing with his own thorn in the flesh, he prayed three times that it would be removed. Although we don't exactly know what Paul's "thorn" was, we do know that it was not removed. Whether it was his eyesight, fear or sexuality pressures, the answer Paul received from the Lord was that "my grace is sufficient for thee, for my strength is made perfect in weakness" (II Cor. 12: 9). Paul's weakness allowed God's strength to be made manifest in his life. On a practical level, this is a difficult lesson to comprehend. The flesh tells us to depend on our strengths. The priority of God's kingdom is just the opposite. The Master uses us in our perceived points of weakness.

We desperately need to have the hidden issues of our hearts

revealed in order to deal with the problem of fear in our lives. Are you riddled with overt fear? Is it possible that you have fears that you have not acknowledged or maybe don't even realize are there? While the Bible does not say it is sin to feel fear, I do believe that it is sinful to be controlled by fear. God is ever trying to put us in a position of trust. How have you dealt with the adversity that has entered your life? God is preparing you for something that is beyond your imagination, if you will trust Him for all of the circumstances of your life. As you deal with adversity in your life, remember Principle No. 2: *God allows adversity to reveal our unknown areas of mistrust.*

PRINCIPAL III: GOD ALLOWS ADVERSITY TO PREPARE CHRISTIANS TO BE FIT VESSELS FOR THE MASTER'S SERVICE

CHAPTER 4
HOW GROWING THROUGH ADVERSITY EMPOWERED JOSEPH TO BE A LEADER WITHOUT PRIDE

"...ye thought evil against me but God meant it unto good, to bring to pass, as it is this day, to save much people alive." Genesis 50: 20

When we think of preparation for a job, we naturally think of schooling or some type of vocational training. If we were to consider the normal criteria for leadership education, work history and talent would be are high on the list. But God's ways are different than our ways and His demands higher than our best intellect can imagine. The Lord puts a high premium on adversity as preparation for leadership. The Bible provides a wonderful example in the life of Joseph of Adversity Principle Number 3: *God Allows Adversity To Prepare Christians To Be Fit Vessels For His Service.*

The prevailing view of Joseph is that he was righteous in all of his ways. The story of this fresh-faced young man, whose character was head-and-shoulders above his generation, is an excellent example of how God uses adversity to shape the character of his chosen. While Joseph was a lad whom God planned to use, he also had some issues in his heart that God first needed to purge.

Although the Bible never directly accuses Joseph of being prideful, a close examination of his early history reveals how he needed the adversity sent his way so that when he assumed a position of authority, he had dealt with this most perilous inner heart sin condition.

Since we are accustomed to viewing Joseph without any scrutiny into his deficiencies, the following examination might present a startling revelation. It is important to view Biblical characters in their humanity so that their experiences relate more closely to our own reality. If we look closely enough, we can see the Bible characters without hiding their flaws.

There is an aspect of Joseph's character development that should be considered under Adversity Principle Number 3, *God Allows Adversity To Prepare Christians To Be Fit Vessels For His Service.* In preparation for a candid examination of the life of Joseph, a thoughtful review of his intriguing story, as found in Genesis 37 through 50, would be helpful.

Our first view of Joseph reveals that his father, Jacob, instilled in him the propensity for pride. Jacob or Israel, as God renamed him, was blessed to have a family that consisted of twelve boys (and a number of girls) that he sired through his wives and handmaidens. In the midst of the blessings of this large family, discord developed in these original "children of Israel." The reason for the family discord? Jacob loved Joseph more than all of his other children.

As parents, God wants us to value and love each of our children in a special way designed for their uniqueness. When one child is esteemed over others, a dysfunction is created that harms the esteemed one as well as the ones who are not so well favored. Once established, family dysfunction provides a framework for contentions and controversies that are not consistent with God's best.

There are two apparent reasons for Jacob's preference for Joseph. First, Joseph was the first child of Rachel, the woman Jacob worked some 14 years to make his wife. The tenderness and love that Jacob had for Rachel coupled with her inability to have a child for a long period of time transferred to a preference for the son he finally had with her.

Second, the Bible reveals that Jacob loved Joseph more because he was the son of his old age. Interestingly, Jacob was even older at the birth of Benjamin, Rachel's younger son, than he had been at the birth of Joseph. The reason that Benjamin was not the favorite was probably because Jacob's beloved Rachel died while giving birth to

Benjamin. I would imagine Benjamin might have even resembled Rachel in appearance. This possibly left a psychological mark that brought Jacob pain whenever he saw the younger Benjamin. Unless carefully considered and brought to the Lord, unresolved inner conflict will incubate into emotional pain. If not handled properly, emotional pain will be passed on to the next generation in some unanticipated ways.

For whatever the reason, Jacob, or Israel, loved Joseph more than all of his other children. He loved him so much that he gave him special privileges such as a beautiful coat of many colors (See Gen. 37:3-4). Through this special treatment of Joseph, Jacob perpetuated a family dysfunction. In order to understand the family of Jacob we must spend some time examining how Jacob himself was reared.

Jacob had suffered in his own life because of the preference his own father Isaac had for Jacob's brother Esau. The fact that Isaac loved Esau more caused Jacob to act out in ways that were detrimental to his own character development. Jacob became a deceiver in order to get what he thought he deserved. The pain of Isaac's preference for Esau negatively shaped the character of Jacob.

We are not told exactly why Isaac was more attracted to Esau than to Jacob. It might have been because Esau, unlike Isaac who had been sheltered during his young life, was a rugged man who preferred the outdoors. Possibly, the axiom that opposites attract was at work here because the disfavored Jacob seemed to be much like his father. For whatever reason, Esau was the father's favorite. Jacob, upon having his own family, had never effectively purged himself of this childhood hurt and this dysfunction affected his own child rearing.

A review of the relationship between the brothers Jacob and Esau reveals that they lived virtually their entire adult lives estranged from one another. The impetuous Esau had unwisely sold his birthright privilege to Jacob for only a bowl of stew during their young adult years. Later, Jacob stole the family blessing from Esau.

When Esau found out about his loss of the family blessing, he was furious and sought to kill his brother. Jacob lived much of his adult life on the run and in mortal fear that Esau would come and take retribution against him for perpetrating this fraud (See Gen. 25: 23-34, 27: 1-46).

This digression is necessary to show that unless a dysfunction is confronted and dealt with it is apt to be passed to the next generation in even more perverse ways. Since Jacob had not completely dealt with his own childhood issues, he repeated the mistake of preference when he had his own family. As we return to the story of Jacob's family we can see how this intergenerational preference had been passed down. The bottom line is that Jacob had a preference for Joseph.

By his favoritism, Jacob not only placed Joseph in a position of pride, he positioned his other children in a posture of resentment, another deep issue of the heart. In order for God to use Joseph he had to cut through the issues in his heart that was fostered by his early treatment by his father. In addition, God was allowing the brothers the opportunity to deal with their own issues of the heart.

When reviewing the situation between Joseph and his brothers, we often consider the disturbing lack of character the brothers displayed by selling their brother into slavery. Seldom do we examine why the characters of these other children of Israel were so faulty.

Most of us remember that Joseph was sold into slavery by his jealous brothers. Of course, it did not help that Joseph had been bringing evil reports against them to their father Jacob (See Gen. 37:2). Finally, when the brothers were alone with Joseph, they were so angry that they wanted to kill him. Judah then suggested that they not kill Joseph but sell him into slavery.

A look at this situation from the eyes of the brothers gives a more realistic view why his brothers sold Joseph to the Ishmaelite merchants. They were caught in a web of anger and jealousy that was not entirely their making.

The level of resentment Jacob had created in the hearts of his children is uncovered as we read that when Joseph's brothers "saw that their father loved him (Joseph) more than all his brothers, they hated him, and could not speak peaceably to him" (Gen. 37: 4). It's not that Joseph's brothers did not speak peaceably with him, but due to the conditions that their father Jacob created, they *could not* speak peaceably with him. In other words, it was beyond their ability to be at peace with Joseph because of this family dysfunction. The brothers' vision toward Joseph was negatively clouded by the unequal treatment of their father.

It is important to consider how Joseph's brothers must have felt in their innermost hearts. Not only was Joseph given special treatment such as the coat of many colors, his life was even more esteemed than theirs. A careful reading of the story reveals another glimpse into how this dysfunction of preference operated in the everyday life of these brothers.

After Jacob had this family, he had the encounter with his brother Esau that he had been avoiding all of his adult life. Upon hearing the news that Esau was approaching, Jacob immediately thought that he and his family were about to receive retribution from the earlier relationship problems. As Esau approached, Jacob arranged his family in the order of their importance to him. Their importance was illustrated by their positioning to the danger. Jacob put the handmaidens and their children foremost, next he put Leah and her children and finally he placed Rachel and Joseph in the back (See Genesis 33:1-2).

Imagine the feeling of the brothers as they witnessed the insult to them and their own mothers as they were placed in harms way. Consider how they must have felt as they witnessed the lack of esteem shown them by their very own father. I would imagine that this blatant example of preference was repeated many times and in many ways in the everyday lives of this "blended" family. While Joseph would have known how much he was loved, consider the feelings of his brothers. Jacob's preference had a detrimental effect on the character of the brothers as well as on the character of Joseph.

This is not to say that Joseph did not have admirable qualities. In fact, Joseph was a person of great substance and character potential who had the special quality of being touched and equipped by God. But he also basked in the special recognition that he received from his father. This situation was causing Joseph to develop traits which, left unresolved, would keep him from being the kind of leader that God needed to fulfill future tasks. Our loving God, who had designed the great potential of Joseph, also knew just what type of adversity it would take to make this gifted person a fit vessel.

Before encountering adversity, Joseph's pride was causing him to misuse his gifts. Rather than using his considerable gifts of discernment to ease the family tension, young Joseph exacerbated the situation by using his gifts in the wrong way and at the wrong time.

For instance, Joseph had a dream about having a sheaf or cluster of grain that was larger than all of his brother's sheaves. This dream indicated that one day his influence would be greater than their influence. Joseph created a problem when he shared this dream with his family. The problem was that by sharing this dream he displayed an insensitivity that is disturbing. Later, when he had another dream where the sun, moon, and eleven stars made obeisance to him he created more problems. This second dream indicated that even his parents along with his brothers would one day bow down to him. By sharing the dreams Joseph was not only breaking his intimacy with God, he was using his gift to exalt himself (See Gen. 37:6-11).

God gave Joseph these dreams in a spirit of intimacy to show him his future ministry to his family. Although a time would come when he would be able to save them from famine, budding pride pushed Joseph to inappropriately share this information. The untimely sharing of this information was not only a breach of intimacy with God, it caused even more animosity and separation from his brothers. We must always endeavor to use our gifts and abilities to further God's plan and to uplift others, but never to exalt self.

Intimacy is born of having an experience with another that is just between those two. The most common example of intimacy is found in the relationship between a husband and wife that God designed for marriage. The intimacy between a husband and wife is developed as they have shared experiences that are just between the two of them. Over time, this intimacy is enhanced as each partner realizes that they can trust their mate to know everything about them. Security comes when each realizes that this information will never be used inappropriately. We should never break this intimacy by sharing with others details that should be reserved within the relationship.

Intimacy with God is much like the marital relationship, only it is even more intimate. God wants to know that he can share with us important and confidential information and that we will not misuse his trust. Our intimacy with God deepens as he reveals more to us and we are able to use that information to build up others as we minister to them. Untimely sharing of information, or the misuse of the intimate knowledge God gives us in order to uplift ourselves, is a betrayal of this special gift. Joseph was misusing his intimacy with

God and this had to be dealt with.

Nevertheless, God had great plans to use Joseph, but it took the adversity of being sold into slavery, as well as later trials and even a prison term, that put him in a position to be available for God's service without the hint of pride or self sufficiency. While it probably seemed to Joseph that he was in the midst of an unfair circumstance, we, as observers, may clearly see how he was being prepared for a greater ministry.

His brothers sold Joseph to these Ishmaelite captors, who then sold him to Potiphar, the captain of Pharaoh's guard. In all of this adversity, the Bible indicates that the Lord was with Joseph. Joseph's presence in the house of Potiphar, a wealthy Egyptian, was a blessing to the household. Everything Joseph touched seemed to prosper. When we love the Lord and are called according to His purpose, God is with us even in the midst of the most difficult of circumstances.

Potiphar's wife, perhaps sensing something special in the young Joseph but being captive to her own lusts, insisted on having an illicit affair with him. Joseph continually resisted her advances. When she made a sexual advance, Joseph ran from her and, as he was getting away, she grabbed his garment. Potiphar's wife used the evidence of this garment against Joseph, stating that he had tried to force himself upon her. Joseph was punished for doing the right and moral thing and he was sent from a comfortable slavery to what seemed to be a more difficult prison. While we must endure difficult situations, we should ever be mindful of how God is delivering us. We should never be appeased with transitional slavery, no matter how comfortable it may seem.

Joseph must have wondered what else could go wrong, especially since he was being persecuted for standing up for God's truth. Again, the Bible shows God was with him, even in prison. During his stint in prison, Joseph was the freest man in Egypt because, despite the outward appearance of adversity, he was being used of God and being prepared for greater service. Interestingly, Joseph was not just sent to any prison but to a place reserved for the King's prisoner's (Gen. 39:20). The only acceptable way to be in prison is where it is reserved for the King of the Universe's prisoners.

Joseph continued to develop the needed skills for his great future as a deliverer while still in prison. Not only was he able to handle this outwardly negative situation, he flourished in it. As observers, we are able to see how the Lord was with Joseph during his adversity. During his imprisonment God showered him with "steadfast love" (Gen. 39:21 NRSV).

The steadfast love of God will be made manifest in our lives during times of adversity when we learn to trust God for the unexplainable. When all seems well and we seem to have no immediate need, we often only pay lip service to the trust relationship with the Lord. During times of adversity, especially when we are unable to "figure out" a conclusion to the perplexity that is present before us, it is the steadfast love of God that will comfort and sustain us. In order to test the integrity of our experience with God, we sometimes must be placed in a position of total trust so that we may have a true measure of where we stand.

Whenever Joseph would reach the depths of discouragement, I believe that he would experience the presence of the living God, and know that he was loved. This love is illustrated in the fact that Joseph did not become bitter with his circumstances and the Lord "gave him favor in the sight of the chief jailer." One indication that we are on the right track in our relationship with God is when we are given favor in unusual and unexpected situations. Let me digress to use a modest personal example of God's favor in the midst of adversity.

My wife and I married while we were still college students. Shortly before our marriage, Joy, my wife, had encountered a very serious illness. She nearly died of a brain aneurysm but through the adversity of her illness we were both brought into a closer personal relationship with the Lord and with each other. After her recovery we both returned to school and shortly thereafter we married. After our marriage, Joy realized that she was not up to college at that time and she worked while I continued in college and worked a couple of part time jobs. As you can imagine, it was difficult to make ends meet and, at the time, I used to joke that our ends had not even been introduced. Nevertheless, our home was filled with the love of God and each other.

One day, while on duty at one of my part time jobs in a local department store chain, the store manager came to my work area and told me of his desire to make me a department manager. This meant I would also have the possibility of later going into the executive management training program. I was thrilled at the prospect of greater income and hope for the future, especially when the store manager indicated that I could work a full time schedule around my college schedule. My exuberance at this prospective management opportunity quickly turned to disappointment when I was informed that I would have to work on the weekend. At this time, all managers had to work every weekend because there was a required manager's meeting.

Now the demand to work on the weekend might seem to be a minor stumbling block, particularly since I could still attend church after the early morning meeting. However, my wife and I had vowed that we would not desecrate the Lord's Day by working our jobs, even if we could still attend church. The store manager was more than a little surprised when I explained to him my great appreciation for the offer, and my admitted great need of the job, but my inability to accept the job because of my faith. I thought that this was the end of the story and started to consider other possible ways out of our financial dilemma. I was disappointed but strangely encouraged as I sensed the steadfast love of God. However, I was still in need of the job and in the same financial condition. I needed an immediate way out.

I was working the evening shift at the store a few days after this job offer, and my refusal to accept based on spiritual grounds. Late in the evening, I received a message over the intercom to report to the store manager's third floor office. Once there, the store manager informed me that he had been thinking about my situation and felt it necessary to explore other options with me. He explained his religious background was as a Lutheran but admitted he did not know much about his own church history. He then said, "Tell me about your church relationship." I first shared with him my understanding of his own church and the great contribution of Martin Luther. He then felt comfortable with inquiring deeper into my situation. "Why," he asked, "would you risk this great opportunity because of a day?" He went on to ask "Couldn't you just go to church after the manager's meeting?"

At that point, I was able to spend a considerable amount of time sharing a Bible study on the call for a Christian to give God the primacy in and through all. It was a thrilling time as I was given an opportunity to share my young faith with this distinguished gentleman.

After we finished the session, I felt that God had opened up this situation as an opportunity for me to share Bible truths. I was also submitted to the idea that losing the opportunity of the job was worth the privilege I had to minister. Importantly, I did not harbor bitterness at the prospective loss of an opportunity and, because of my stand for truth, I believe that God gave me favor in the store manager's sight. I didn't realize at the time that God was not finished with this situation. A few days later a memorandum was received informing the staff that the day for the manager's meeting had been changed to a weekday and that I was appointed to be a new department manager.

You see, what seemed like the disappointment of facing an adverse situation had a twofold purpose in God's plan. First, it allowed me to show my faith by allowing God to lead me through a difficult situation. By showing faith, I allowed God to work His perfect will for my life at that time. I recall this minor situation of adversity and it strengthens me whenever I am faced with an uncomfortable choice of standing for truth.

Second, the situation allowed me to minister in the work environment in a way I would have never imagined yet I still received the job for which I had prayed. The witness was to the Store Manager as well as my fellow employees. Interestingly, after this incident, some of the other managers thanked me for paving the way to have the manager's meeting moved away from the weekend. It was through the "favor" God provided for me that many other employees were blessed to spend additional time with their families and have whole weekends off. God provides favor when we are operating within his perfect will for our lives.

God will give us favor in the midst of the negative circumstances when we commit ourselves to His will. This favor is God's way of easing the burden of the adversity while allowing us to receive the full instruction that we need.

Through all of the great disappointment that Joseph must have felt, God continually indicated His presence to Joseph by the favor shown him. Importantly, through all of the situations, Joseph continued to grow because he did not harbor bitterness.

Joseph's lack of bitterness during the crisis is important because he was able to be blessed by the adversity that came his way while God worked out the issues hidden in his heart. He learned through his adversity that God was ultimately in control and could be trusted for all of the issues of life.

God first gave Joseph favor with Potiphar, then, after he was committed unjustly to jail, additional favor with the jailer. Joseph's favor with the chief jailer was so strong that we are informed the jailer "committed to Joseph's care all the prisoners who were in prison and whatever was done there, he (Joseph) was the one who did it . . . and whatever he did, the Lord made it to prosper" (Gen. 39:22-23). The more Joseph trusted God, the more ministry opportunities he encountered in the midst of the adversity.

After he was in prison and had found favor there, Joseph was able to minister to Pharaoh's chief baker and chief cupbearer who were in prison and out of favor with the King. Apparently these officials of Pharaoh's court had been accused of some type of serious crime against the Kingdom. The importance of the chief baker and cupbearer is because they both had position that dealt with the well being of the ruler.

While in prison with Joseph, both of these former high officials had perplexing dreams that Joseph interpreted. Joseph was able to use his ministry gifts in this most unlikely of circumstances. When the chief baker told his dream to Joseph, the interpretation of the dreams was not encouraging. Joseph informed the baker that within three days he would lose his life through execution.

Joseph's ministry to the baker was crucial. Although the Bible does not give us details into the relationship between the baker and Joseph, a person who had Joseph's relationship with God must have shared the good news of God's love. Through Joseph, the baker would have had an opportunity to obtain a salvation experience with God before his death. We are placed in situations for ministry. In fact, many times our greatest ministry opportunities come when we are in the midst of the storm and must utilize the reprieve of helping others to take us away from our own problems. True ministry will focus on the needs of others and will ultimately put our own situation in its proper perspective.

When the cupbearer explained his dream to Joseph the

interpretation was much more encouraging. The cupbearer was to be returned to his former high position in Pharaoh's Court. In exchange for providing this encouraging news to the cupbearer, Joseph only had one request. He requested that when the cupbearer was restored to his position that he would tell Pharaoh of his wrongful imprisonment and sojourn of being stolen out of the land of the Hebrews.

While the request seemed perfectly reasonable, it was indicative of Joseph jumping ahead of God again. It was reminiscence of the time when Joseph prematurely shared his dreams of prominence with his family. One writer suggested that when Joseph asked to be remembered he caused himself additional time in prison.[1] Whatever the reason, the cupbearer did not remember Joseph after he returned to the king's service until "two whole" years later.

Imagine the potential for bitterness that Joseph must have encountered for those two long years. Again, we do not see any trace of bitterness in Joseph. Joseph patience can now be credited to his reliance on the Lord. Not only had he been sold into slavery, he was in prison unjustly and now forgotten by a person he had helped. What Joseph did not naturally know, but had to accept by faith, was that God was still working out his circumstances.

Joseph's lack of bitterness during his adversity is important because God was able to move him to the next level of discipleship. Joseph learned to surrender the hidden issues of his heart to God's healing power. In addition, Joseph learned through this adversity experience that God was ultimately in control of his life. When we submit to God's control of our lives, the best is always yet to come. Always remember that the best is yet to come.

It is important to note that when it came time for Joseph to enter into the accomplishment phase of his life, he was a man thoroughly prepared for service. Remember the dream that Pharaoh had of seven fatted calves followed by seven lean calves? The lean calves then turned and ate the fatted calves. Pharaoh later had a correlated dream of seven plump and good ears of grain that were followed by seven thin and blighted ears of corn. The seven thin ears of corn, like the

---

[1]For a full discussion on the story of Joseph, see Kendall, R.T. , *God Meant it for Good: A Fresh Look at the Life of Joseph*. Charlotte, NC: Morningstar Publications , 1986.

thin calves, devoured the seven plump ears.

Pharaoh needed someone to explain the dream but the court seers and magicians failed. After two long years at a time of great need for the kingdom of Egypt, the cupbearer finally remembered Joseph, who, by the way, was still housed in the King's prison. The earlier lack of memory by the cupbearer was undoubtedly providentially inspired.

Had the cupbearer remembered earlier, Joseph would not have completed the adversity experience needed to be totally stripped of pride. Interestingly, the time spent in Potiphar's household and in prison allowed Joseph to learn the language and customs of Egypt, which would later be needed for him to rule. Importantly, the thrilling scene had to be set for the dramatic saving of Egypt and Israel. Remember Adversity Principle 3: *God allows adversity to prepare Christians to be fit vessels for the Master's service.*

Joseph was suddenly called upon to deliver a word of explanation to Pharaoh. After all the time of waiting and growing, Joseph was now in the center stage that God had foretold. He was being prepared all these many years for this time of unexpected service.

The mature Joseph's growth was shown as he was recounting and explaining Pharaoh's dream that seven years of plenty would be followed by seven years of famine. However, this time Joseph did not insert his own dreams. He said nothing about his own situation or the dreams he had about a personal rise to power. Joseph only spoke the information necessary to deliver God's message to Pharaoh because he had learned to "let go" and "let God." Before the adversity experience, Joseph's response would have undoubtedly been much different. He probably would have given Pharaoh the interpretation of his dream, but then also found a way to recount his own dreams and injustices to Pharaoh.

Through the adversity principle, Joseph learned that God was in control and he was to serve without any hint of self-sufficiency. God was now able to use Joseph beyond his wildest imagination with the assurance that Joseph's ministry would not be limited by pride.

Joseph told Pharaoh of the impending crises and suggested that an organization was needed to meet the test. Commissioners should be appointed to mandate the recovery of a portion of the grain during the good years and the distribution to the people during the bad.

Joseph also informed Pharaoh that it was important that a person of the utmost abilities be appointed to oversee this project. In a surprising move that shows God's control even over the King's heart, Pharaoh promoted a lowly slave with only the status of a prisoner of the Most High God, to the position of Prime Minister of the greatest kingdom on earth. This is an amazing illustration of God's leading and ultimate authority over the details of our lives.

Once Joseph was in authority, he did not display any overt bitterness over his past, but he also continued to work through the residual issues of his heart. For instance, after his rise to the post of Prime Minister, Joseph had two children by Asenath the daughter of Potipherah, Priest of On. Although he did not lose his trust in God during the adversity, or even show external bitterness, Joseph had to finally let go of the residual vestiges of internal hurt. The names selected for his children reveal the finality of his healing.

He named his sons Manassah and Ephraim. Joseph invoked the name Manassah for his firstborn to show that "God has made me forget all my hardship and all my father's house." This did not indicate that he had no remembrance of his childhood or of his parents and brothers, it simply meant that he would no longer be bound by any negative emotions over his brothers' betrayal. It was also evidence that he would no longer be limited by the family dysfunction of his father's household.

Joseph named his second son Ephraim, which was an emblem of thanksgiving for the fruitfulness that God had given him in the land of his misfortunes. The time of affliction and trial flowered into a blessing for Joseph, his family and the history of Israel. The adversity of Joseph is now understood to be the channel that provided deliverance for Israel and the preservation of the seed line of Jesus Christ.

When the famine in the land foretold by Pharaoh's dream became a reality, Jacob's family was also affected. As the famine induced deprivation increased, Father Jacob sent the brothers to the Egypt, now well prepared by Joseph, for provisions. Joseph was able to handle the experience of being in control of his brothers' fate without bitterness, pride or retribution. After testing them to make sure they had truly changed, Joseph revealed himself to his brothers in one of the most emotional scenes in recorded history.

One cannot help but be moved with how Joseph related to his brothers after they were now under his control in Egypt. He embraced his brothers and informed them that they should not be grieved or angry with themselves for their part in the events. With tears in his eyes and emotion in his voice, Joseph was able to testify that "God did send me before you to preserve life" (Gen. 45:5). What a wonderful experience when a person of influence has a heart that is ordered after God's will and has been regenerated by submission to God's intervention. Joseph was a person whom God could use because his heart was no longer infected with the sin of pride.

Joseph could have been brought into Egypt to fulfill this mission in a myriad of ways but, in His divine omniscience, God knew that the adversity trip was the best for all concerned. Look at the net result. Jacob was placed face to face with how he had favored his one son over the others, and given an opportunity to repent. The brothers learned the lessons of sowing and reaping and were forced to confront their own sinful hearts and repent. And Joseph became a leader without a peer because he had dealt with the issue of pride and learned the lessons of absolute trust. God is so good, in fact it is the "goodness of God that leads us to repentance" (Romans 2:4).

We must understand how God is with us, even during the dark days of adversity. Imagine how Joseph must have felt during those years in prison. At times Joseph must have thought that God had abandoned him. Had Joseph become bitter during those dark years, God would not have been able to use him in this magnificent way. Many of us forfeit the benefit that living through adversity produces because we fail to embrace God during those dark hours. When we fail to embrace God during our adversity experiences we limit our availability to be used for greater tasks. If we can just focus on the goodness of God during times of adversity, we can avoid the bitterness that leads to spiritual ruin.

Imagine the result if Joseph had harbored and been blinded by resentment during his time of slavery and imprisonment. He would have missed the blessing for which he was being prepared. We must never allow adversity to make us bitter as we move from the past experience to God's current blessing.

For instance, when Joseph was in a place of prominence, he did not allow the past to keep him from assisting his family and the quality of his life was reflective of his selflessness. There is a reason that we are in our family of origin. When God particularly blesses one person in the family, that blessing is given in order to bless the greater family. Unfortunately, many people do not experience the happiness that material blessings can bring because they become selfish and self-serving.

Some very successful people have tried to separate their personal business and wealth from their extended family. They ultimately struggle with issues of fulfillment and happiness. Many try to manipulate family relationships with their wealth that would have been natural absent their self-centered position.

All of the issues of our hearts must be considered for the potential for pride, as we trust God to lead us as we do our entrusted work. While we often hold on to our "issues" for personal satisfaction, God is endeavoring to improve us through adversity if we, like Joseph, will just surrender the issues of our hearts and trust Him.

God is attempting to reveal the sin issues of our hearts, of which we often have no conscious knowledge. The adversity principles are designed in order to bring to the surface every hidden heart issue and every innermost problem that plagues us. We need to be stripped in order to be totally naked but without shame before the searcher of our heart. We must distill our relationship to a level of total trust.

While modern presumptions teach that the way to fulfillment is through self-love and prosperity, the Bible instructs us that we are only fulfilled when we are within the Sovereign will of God for our lives. When we die to ourselves, we can live for the greater good of God's will. We should internalize the lessons of Adversity Principle Number 3: *God allows adversity to prepare Christians to be fit vessels for His service.* Joseph needed to be exposed, through adversity, to his own propensity for pride before he could be used as a fit vessel. An examination of foundations of pride will allow us to better see why we must not harbor this dangerous inner heart malady.

CHAPTER 5
THE PROBLEM WITH PRIDE

"Pride goeth before destruction and a haughty spirit before a fall."
Proverbs 16: 18

    A compelling area of "Theodicy" is the examination of the origins of sin. While it is sometimes difficult to understand human suffering in light of asserting that God is good, it can also be difficult to explain why evil was originally allowed to develop. An examination of how evil originally surfaced helps us to better understand God's continuing admonitions against pride. When we harbor pride, we are unwittingly aligning ourselves with a movement against God that is far beyond the simple acts of being prideful.

    Pride, like fear, is a problem that is found in the innermost recesses of the heart. While the true effect of pride can be more difficult to identify than fear, pride is also an indication of a lack of trust in God. In fact, the proud trust in their own wisdom and power which limits their ability to be used as vessels of honor. Rather than being fully used by God, the proud are in a position to be resisted by Him who knows the issues of the heart (See James 4:6 and I Peter 5:5).

    One reason pride is so objectionable is because it goes to the core of our spiritual relationship. Pride can masquerade as some other non-offensive trait such as zeal or be present in those who seem to have God's blessings because of their position or material wealth. Importantly, pride is a form of idolatry because we take credit for those things the Lord has provided. Adversity Principle Number 3 is custom designed for those who have hearts that are being soiled by pride: *God allows adversity to prepare Christians to be fit vessels for His service.*

Most importantly, pride is so unacceptable because it is born of the root of self-sufficiency. Apart from God we have nothing because our very life is from the fountain of the Creator's love. With God in our lives, we must only acknowledge His goodness, mercy, and grace as the source of who we are and what we have. Whenever we are tempted to look to self through pride we should consider how we are showing that Satan rather than God is leading in our lives. The roots of pride are worth considering.

Before pride developed in Lucifer, every created being was in perfect conformity to the will of the Creator. Every being directed their heart and energy to the worship of the Creator God and the fulfillment of His will. In this perfect universe, no individual focused on personal needs but only on fulfilling the perfect will of the Creator. All were directed toward unity of purpose as the Creator met all their needs. Awareness centered on the Creator and His goodness, majesty, and leading, which, in turn, gave each individual purpose as they conformed to the Master's perfect plan. This perfect structure made life completely fulfilling because each individual was totally available for service.

It is amazing that in the mist of this wonderful perfection, where every creature had legitimate purpose, a devil mysteriously developed. The mystery of iniquity arose when Lucifer, whose name means "light bearer", and who stood in the presence of God, thought that his beauty and close position to the Creator somehow entitled him to also be the object of praise and worship. While we are not told exactly why pride arose in this "perfect" being, we know that he became "self-aware." The curtain, which obscures the mystery of iniquity, is drawn open to allow us to examine a Biblical discourse concerning Satan. The texts are worth considering in their entirety:

> "How art thy fallen from heaven, O Lucifer, son of the morning! how art thy cut down to the ground, which dist weaken the nations!
>
> "For thou (Lucifer) hast said in thine heart, I will ascend into heaven, I will exalt my throne above the stars of God; I will sit also upon the mount of the congregation, in the sides of the north. I will ascend above the heights of the clouds; I will be like the most High" (Isa. 14:12-14).

The Bible then provides the origin and future destiny of the fallen Lucifer in verity:

"Yet thou shalt be brought down to hell, to the sides of the pit." (Isa. 14:15).

> Thou hast been in Eden the garden of God; every precious stone was thy covering, the sardus, topaz, and the diamond, the beryl, the onyx, and the jasper, the sapphire, the emerald, and the carbuncle, and gold: the workmanship of thy tabrets and of thy pipes was prepared in thee the day that thou wast created.
> Thou art the anointed cherub that covereth; and I have set thee so; thou wast upon the holy mountain of God; thou hast walked up and down in the mist of the stones of fire. Thou wast perfect in thy ways from the day that thou wast created, till iniquity was found in thee.
> By the multitude of thy merchandise they have filled the midst of thee with violence; and thou hast sinned; therefore I will cast thee as profane out of the mountain of God: and I will destroy thee, O covering cherub, from the midst of the stones of fire.
> Thine heart was lifted up because of thy beauty, thou hast corrupted thy wisdom by reason of thy brightness: I will cast thee to the ground, I will lay thee before kings, that they may behold thee.
> Thou hast defiled thy sanctuaries by the multitudes of thine iniquities, by the iniquity of thy traffick; therefore will I bring forth a fire from the midst of thee, it shall devour thee, and I will bring thee to ashes upon the earth in the sight of all them that behold thee.
> All they that know thee among the people shall be astonished at thee; thou shalt be a terror, and never thou shalt thou be any more. (Eze. 28:12-19)

This is an amazing explanation of how pride led to the fall of Lucifer. Lucifer was created perfect. He was a beautiful, talented and anointed cherub. As a covering cherub, he was always allowed to be in the immediate presence of God. Not only was Lucifer covered with every precious stone, he was an extraordinary musician. His body contained internal pipes and tabrets (tambourines).

Lucifer apparently fell in love with himself as he started to display his beauty and lavish covering. He gradually failed to acknowledge God as the source of all of his gifts. His praise turned inward to the point that he eventually thought that he, rather than God, should be the object of praise. All of the endowments furnished to this wonderful creature by our loving Creator were now turned to selfishness as Lucifer perverted these gifts.

For instance, the internal pipes and tambourines that Lucifer was provided so he could be music-worship-leader were eventually used to exalt self rather than to sing praises to the only One who is worthy. The precious stones that God provided to cover the exterior of Lucifer were also perverted, as the creature Lucifer pointed to himself rather than to the Gift Giver, Creator God. Lucifer came to love and esteem himself so much that he would rather display himself and his gifts rather than to use the gifts in praise and honor of the Gift Giver.

These gifts were all perverted from the selflessness of God's kingdom to a kingdom built on a foundation of selfishness and pride. He was fully equipped for worship but somehow became self-aware. This simple act of self-awareness flowered into self-importance that drifted into pride, finally making the once-perfect Lucifer an unholy devil. Lucifer fell from a position in a kingdom built on love and selflessness to lead a kingdom built and operated on the principles of pride and selfishness that leads to sin.

It is important that the love of display continues to be symptomatic of those who have been lifted up by pride. In the not so distant past, Christians were known for modesty and simplicity of life style. Virtually every denomination and sect had theological admonitions limiting, if not completely prohibiting the use of jewelry, colorful cosmetics and lavish clothing. Those who ignored these admonitions were compared to Jezebel.

Jezebel was the wicked wife of King Ahab. Ahab allowed the Kingdom of Israel to sink into idolatry and worldliness during his reign. Jezebel epitomized a lavish and selfish lifestyle and was known for her "worldly" use of colorful cosmetics and ornamentation. Her excesses were indicative of Israel at a time of idolatry and detachment from God.

Increasingly, the modern Christian community seems to have no standards when it comes to worldliness in dress and lifestyle. Whatever the worldly style of the day might be, it seems the church now follows without qualification and to even mentioned the Biblical admonition of modesty seems pharisaical. When the world wears inappropriate clothing, the church follows and it is becoming increasingly difficult to tell the Christian from the "world." The doctrines of self-love and prosperity have provided a moral foundation for these types of excesses as the Christian community focuses on self rather than the historical purity of the gospel.

It is true that many of the old denominational admonitions against the use of these items had the Christian community much to involved in the externals that leads to legalism. This is not a call to return to legalistic formulations of any kind nor is it an attempt to label anyone as a Jezebel. Christ taught us to put our focus on the internal rather than the externals when He accused the Pharisees of being "whited sepulchers (or bleached tombs)": clean on the outside but on the inside full of dead men's bones. However, our internal condition is eventually reflected in our external manifestations and we should examine ourselves to see what part pride plays in our lives. Granted, the issue is larger than what we wear, but we should be very careful that we do not align ourselves with Satan's rebellion against God.

Since his expulsion from heaven, Satan has been leading a rebellion against God's selfless kingdom. He intends to deceive all of the created beings into self-awareness and self-motivation. He aims for as many as possible to join him in his kingdom of selfishness, rather than being selflessly inspired and actualized by the Creator God. He has been amazingly successful. One third of the heavenly host followed his deception. Even father Adam and mother Eve bought into the deception in the Garden of Eden. While we haven't been given a complete picture of how members of the angelic hosts were deceived, we have a clearer view of what happened in the garden (See Gen. 2:15-25; 3:1-19).

Adam and Eve were placed in a perfectly equipped garden with only one limitation; do not eat from the tree of the knowledge of good and evil. Through the deception of the serpent, Eve and Adam appropriated for themselves the fruit that was forbidden. The deception that Satan used to beguile Eve was twofold. First, he told her that if she ate of the fruit she would not die, which was in direct contravention to what God had said (Gen. 2: 17; 3:4). The doctrine that the sinner will never die has pervaded the Christian community and is a continuation of this original lie. The Bible informs us that only God has immortality, and thus our hope for everlasting life, in any form, is found only in Him.

The doctrine of the ever-burning hell contradicts the goodness of God. While the fires of hell will be real, it will only be until the sinner is consumed for their sins. There is a growing movement of what is known as annihilationism led by such mainstream evangelicals as theologians John Stott, Clark Pinnock, John Wenham and Edward Fudge.[2] The subject of annihilation in no ways minimizes the great gulf of relationship and other loss that the sinner will engender by missing the blessing of God's eternal kingdom. But God, in his infinite mercy, will not allow an eternal punishing for a lifetime of sin.

Many have gone to their graves defying God's goodness based upon the erroneous belief that an ever-burning Hell would be unjust. Others, considering the myth that Satan would be in charge of hell could not grasp the absurdity that a just God would allow the devil to be in charge of His justice system.

The Biblical truth regarding the punishment of the wicked, is that God will destroy the sinner, but even his punishments are meted out in love. Those who refuse the saving mercy of God will receive their

---

[2] John Stott, in the Anglican church and author of *Evangelical Essentials*, 1988. pages 313-320; Clark Pinnock, *The Destruction of the Finally Impenitent*, 1990; John Wenham *see The Goodness of God*, 1974; *Universalism and the Doctrine of Hell*, 1991, chapter 6: *The Case for Conditional Immortality;* Edward Fudge, *The Fire That Consumes, A Biblical and Historical Study of Final Punishment,* Houston, Texas: Providential Press, 1982.

just rewards in the fires of hell, but when they have been punished according to their works they will be no more. The real punishment will be their lack of inclusion in the eternal home of the righteous, where, even if allowed in, it would be a miserable, uncomfortable experience for them.

Can you imagine one who has the motivation of selfishness in the corridors of a kingdom built on selflessness and devotion to God? Heaven and the "earth made new" will be a place where holiness and selflessness abound. The unregenerate sinner would find no peace or comfort in this environment. I remember one preacher making the humorous observation that sinners in heaven would be digging up the streets of gold to hoard them for themselves.

The unrighteous will not eternally live, but this destruction is borne out of the love of the Creator God, hallowed be His Holy name. The wicked will be ashes under the feet of the righteous and they will not be allowed to live forever because the "...wages of sin is death but the gift of God is everlasting life" (See Mal. 4: 1-4, Rom. 6:23, Rom. 2:6,7, I Cor. 15: 52-54).

The perception of hell that suggests that Satan will be in charge and sinners will either be able to continue in their sinful lifestyle, or be under the dominion and punishment of Satan forever is also erroneous. The Bible truth is that Satan will not be in charge of hell, and the Ezekiel text indicates that the fires of hell will come forth from the midst of the original wicked one (Eze. 28-18). This is a fitting end to Satan and sin, because the sin problem started from the pride found in the midst of the once-perfect Lucifer. The fires of purification will come from the same heart where the problem started.

The second lie, or really a half-truth, that Satan told Adam and Eve, was that God did not want them to eat of the fruit because He knew that their eyes would be opened and they would be as gods (Gen.3:5). Although God did not wish for their eyes to be open to the knowledge of good and evil, it was a limitation placed on them for their own good. The Creator knew that this knowledge would result in pain, suffering, and sorrow and would ultimately set His creatures apart from Him. Rather than having the filter for knowledge that God would lovingly provide, the eating of the fruit gave them, and now us, direct inclusion in the good and evil process.

Eating the forbidden fruit from the tree of knowledge was humanity's entry portal to the deception of self-love. By their disobedience our first parents became self-aware. Rather than focusing on God and others, they now focused on themselves. They became aware that they were naked and attempted to clothe themselves with fig leaves. They blamed each other and God for their sins and, most importantly, they hid from God.

Self-love is part of the self-awareness that will make us attempt to clothe ourselves with our own works as Adam and Eve attempted to clothe themselves with the fig leaves. When we focus on ourselves, we will fashion a covering that is not of God every time. The Biblical goals for the Christian is not to become aware of, preserve, or even love ourselves. The Christian is instructed that if we are to be children of God we must die to ourselves.

The Apostle Paul taught us that we must die to ourselves when he informs us that we must die daily (I Cor. 15:31). Why would we allow ourselves to die when the modern goal is to love ourselves? The question then arises, if we should not love ourselves how should we feel about ourselves? Should we practice self-deprecation, self-flagellation or even suicide? The answer is an emphatic <u>NO</u>. We should not practice self anything! We have worth, intrinsic worth born of our relationship with our Creator God. And because of this relationship we are a part of something much greater than ourselves. When people do not realize this foundational point, they enter into behaviors that are self-defeating. Self-love is a counterfeit for the true validation of God's love. The self-love theory makes us postulate wrong solutions to our problems and these solutions are not according to God's word.

For instance, suicide is often thought of as a result of a lack of self-love. I have even heard it taught that borne out of this lack of love for self, people commit this most heinous act. The truth is that suicide is the epitome of selfishness. The person who commits this unspeakable act is not interested in the effect that this selfish act will have on others, they only focus, inappropriately, on their own perception of pain and disillusionment. Yet, the modern self-love theory teaches that these people needed to love themselves more. Wrong premises will provide wrong solutions every time.

As we die to ourselves and allow Christ, who is our

righteousness, to dwell in us, we can only then truly live for the purpose of God. We don't have to buy into the self-love dichotomy when we know God, the only One who can truly give worth, esteems us. Because of our connection with God we become joint heirs to the universal truth of love. We don't have to spend time preserving ourselves, God, through Christ, will preserve us as we learn the lesson of trust and dependence.

Armed with the understanding that God himself created us and this same God, through Jesus Christ, redeemed us, we will be *God actualized* and motivated rather then *self-actualized* and self motivated. To preserve ourselves is not a very worthy goal but, by dying to self, we open the door to the ministry of God flowing in and through our lives.

When we realize that we are not bound by circumstances the door opens for God to use us for ministry as we lean fully on Him. Only when the Christian community wakes up to the deception of self-love and self-focus, will we return to the primitive gospel that is needed to finish the work of the great commission. Every member of the Christian community minding the matters of others, every member esteeming others better then themselves, every person walking in and being led by the Spirit of the living God is the way the Church was designed to operate. We must allow ourselves to be purged of the taint of self before we can be fully used as vessels of honor, fit for the Master's service.

We must not harbor pride, in any form, if we expect to be fully used by the Father. We have examined how God must empty us of ourselves before he can fully use us through the life and ministry of Joseph. The utilization of the adversity principle in Joseph's life provides an amazing example of how God purged him in order to prepare him for an amazing ministry. When Joseph conquered self by dying to self, he became a powerful force in the hands of the Living God. Are you ready to allow yourself to be emptied through the adversity principle so that God can use you for this special work?

Remember Adversity Principle Number 3: *God allows adversity to prepare Christians to be fit vessels for His service.* The next principle is related. In order to use us in His wonderful plan, Adversity Principle Number 4: *God allows adversity to teach Christians the lessons of trust* is invoked.

PRINCIPAL IV: GOD ALLOWS ADVERSITY TO TEACH CHRISTIANS THE LESSONS OF TRUST

CHAPTER 6
HOW GOD USED ADVERSITY TO HEAL MOSES' LACK OF TRUST

"And Moses answered and said, but, behold, they will not hearken unto my voice: for they will say, the Lord hath not appeared unto to thee." Exodus 4:1

Do you believe that you are being molded for some future task, yet it seems it is taking so long perhaps you missed your calling? Take heart, God needs special people to fulfill his will and He works patiently with us until we are ready for our assignment. Let's consider an example of God's patience in preparing a person for a special task.

God needed a man to complete a mission that has never quite been duplicated. Imagine reading the want ads for this position: WANTED: 1) a leader schooled in the strategic movement of millions of men, women and children and their necessary provisions in a desert environment; 2) a General proficient in the art of warfare, who could teach untrained and undisciplined men to fight; 3) a skilled politician and judge of human nature to deal with millions of people whose identity had been either lost or corrupted during 430 years of slavery; 4) a person so approachable that he would be known as the meekest man on earth; 5) a person so caring that he would be willing to have his name taken out of the book of life to save his followers, and finally; 6) a person so bold in nature yet pure in heart so that he would be able to talk one on one with God.

This job description certainly narrowed the field of appropriate applicants. Although there was a perfect candidate for this job, he had character traits that needed to be eliminated before he could start his ministry. It took eighty years for these character impediments to be conquered enough for him to be in the position for which he had been called.

The story of Moses is a prime example of a person whom God chose, but one who also had issues hidden deep within the recesses of his heart. These issues had to be exposed before he could be fully engaged in his God-ordained ministry. Moses' life is illustrative of the Fourth Principle of Adversity: *God allows adversity to teach Christians the lessons of trust.*

The great Moses was born into a slavery environment that was made even more difficult by Pharaoh's decree to kill every male born to Hebrew parents. (See Exodus Chapters 1-6 for the story of Moses' early life). In this unpleasant situation, Moses' parents were blessed with this "goodly child." In order to preserve his life, Moses' parents had to hide him for three months.

It must have been very difficult in the household of Amram and Jochebed during the pregnancy and first months of Moses' life. Imagine the trauma created for this family as they hid a pregnancy and later a newborn child for this period of time. Moses' prenatal experience must have been impacted because Jochebed would have been under extreme stress while certainly hiding her pregnancy. She must have been, at the very least, full of trepidation that her child would be born male. It has been shown that the shaping of our trust starts when we are in the womb, and Moses did not have a very good start. Further, rather than the joy and sense of community that normally surrounds the birth of a new child, baby Moses was hidden away in order to keep him from the authorities that wanted to kill him.

At his birth, there was no loving community embrace for Moses, no rush of communal joy during the first months of his life. Moses' parents might have been forced to stifle his cries when visitors were in the house or when the authorities made their examination and searches for compliance to the law. He might have been, through necessity, ignored and possibly left alone for long periods of time. At the very least, Moses must have felt the tension that surrounded his presence in the household, even though he was greatly loved.

After being hidden for three months Moses was put in an ark and left alone in the water while his sister stood afar off. It was then that Moses was taken by Pharaoh's daughter and raised as her own. It is interesting to note that when Pharaoh's daughter first saw the baby Moses he was weeping (see Ex. 2:6).

Children learn trust and self worth through early experiences with their parents and from the events that form their early environment. Divine providence shaped circumstances, so that Moses was then given back to his birth mother, Jochebed, to be nursed, but it is more than plausible that the first crucial weeks of Moses life did not place him in an environment of trust.

Moses was reared in the house of Pharaoh, the most powerful ruler on Earth at that time. At the age of forty he left the comforts of Pharaoh's house because he no longer wished to be known as the son of Pharaoh's daughter. He then aligned himself with his Hebrew kindred, following the call that he knew God had on his life.

The circumstances surrounding his birth and upbringing probably meant that Moses was never really known or embraced by the Hebrew community. In addition, his sudden, questionable entrance into the house of Pharaoh probably meant that he never quite fit in the Egyptian community as well. A person who is not well adjusted into their community environment is inclined to have issues of self-worth and trust. But what man sees as dysfunction, God can heal and use according to his purpose.

It was with a heart conditioned by his early environment that Moses entered into what he must have felt was the calling on his life. After being raised in the household of Pharaoh, in line to become Pharaoh himself, Moses became increasingly aware that his calling was greater than being a part of Egyptian royalty. Unfortunately, because of the issues of his heart, he was not ready to take the mantle of servant leadership and it would take Adversity Principle Number 4: *God allows adversity to teach Christians the lessons of trust* to make Moses the man God needed him to be.

When we view Moses at forty years of age, after his acknowledgment of his Hebrew heritage, we find him attempting to start a ministry to his people through force. Moses had tried to minister to his people by taking matters into his own hands. By killing an Egyptian involved in a dispute with one of his fellow Hebrews, Moses operated in his own strength while failing to wait on God.

Importantly, the innermost issues of his heart were of patience and trust, not hatred and malice. Had Moses' issue been hate or malice I believe that God would have dealt with him differently. The issue Moses had with trust may have come from the facts surrounding his birth and early life (See Ex. 2:1-10).

Because of his innermost heart issues, he operated in the wrong way and according to the laws of the wrong kingdom. The lesson for us is that anything less than a full leaning on God is unacceptable and, in the long run, unproductive. God lovingly used adversity to prepare Moses for his future ministry. Moses needed the lessons of patience, which, in turn, led him to trust God through surrender.

The Bible is careful to record that Moses tried to avenge the wrong perpetrated by an Egyptian on one of his Hebrew brethren in secret (Ex.2:11-14, Acts 7:25-28). After seeing that no man was looking, Moses slew an Egyptian who had wronged one of his fellow Hebrews. He actually thought that no one knew of his crime. Later, when he was trying to be a peacemaker between two of his Hebrew brethren, he was surprised that other people knew of his earlier crime. One of them asked him, "Who made you judge over us, are you going to kill us like you killed the Egyptian."

Moses, born in secrecy and reared in a lie, thought he could kill in secret and get away with it in order to do God's will. He needed to confront the secrecy and lies that had surrounded his early life. Moses had "unfinished business" that he needed to deal with so that he could be a fit vessel of honor for the Master's service.

On a practical basis, one can only imagine the whispers and jealousies in the royal entourage about this "son" of Pharaoh's daughter, born to her without a pregnancy. How many lies must have been told to perpetuate the myth and the ambiguities that it must have created in Moses' heart. Moses needed time to reflect on his life and allow God to show him who he really was. The adversity route proved invaluable to the growth in grace that Moses needed to fulfill God's purpose for his life.

Moses found himself an acknowledged murderer and a fugitive

from justice. All of the secrets of his life were now out in the open and he probably wanted to get as far away from Egypt as he could. He had undoubtedly heard the whispers in the court of Pharaoh that he was not really the grandson of the ruler. He had probably also felt the pain of not being accepted by the Hebrew slaves whom he knew to be his ethnic brothers.

Moses left Egypt and took refuge with a simple Midian family. It took some forty years of being in the Midian desert tending to his father-in-law's flock before Moses learned to fully deal with the issues of his heart and to develop the patience and trust that would allow him to be the man that God needed to fulfill His purpose. Moses' life is a prime example of Adversity Principle Number 4: *God allows adversity to teach Christians the lessons of trust.*

After forty years of tending sheep, God suddenly spoke to Moses from a bush that was burning but not consumed by the fire. The Lord told Moses that it was time for him to take the mantle of leadership for his people. It was now time for Moses to go back to Egypt to complete the ministry he had started forty years before.

When finally confronted by God for ministry, Moses revealed the esteem issues that caused him to have a lack of trust. Moses asked God, "Who am I, that I should go unto Pharaoh?" (Ex. 3:11) Here was Moses, a man who literally grew up in the household of Pharaoh, one who was schooled in all of the ways of Egyptian royalty, yet he did not think himself able to represent God before Pharaoh. Of all people on earth, his early circumstances and relationship with the royal family made him the perfect person for God to use in this particular circumstance.

Moses was forced to confront the trust issues and to surrender himself to what God was asking him to do. The adversity of forty years in the Midian desert as well as the forty additional years in the wilderness while leading God's people taught Moses the everyday lessons that God can be trusted. But in Moses' weakness, God's strength was made perfect.

The Bible informs us that Moses was one of the meekest men that ever walked the earth. Meekness became one of Moses greatest attributes although it had probably always been considered a weakness. Moses' meekness probably developed because of his early life dysfunction, yet he was used of God through the point of his perceived weakness.

While the years in the wilderness might have solved Moses problems with patience, he still needed to know that he was God's man and that he could trust God to equip him for the ministry he was being asked to perform. Moses finally must have been convinced that his background was appropriate for the presentation needed in Egypt, but he also had to be convinced that the Hebrews would accept him. He told God that the Children of Israel would not believe him and would not hearken to his voice (Exodus 4:1). Even after being told by God that all of this would be taken care of Moses told God of his slowness of speech as another excuse, which in reality is another trust issue. Moses was allowing himself to be limited by the fact that he stuttered.

The fact that Moses speech was impaired by a stutter is even more indication that he had unresolved childhood issues. Many who encounter early childhood trauma develop an inability to communicate appropriately though speech. Moses had carried this childhood impediment with him his entire life. He felt limited by it and eventually asked God to allow him to take his brother Aaron as his mouthpiece.

God's response to Moses is revealing. When Moses informed God that he was "slow of Speech" God responded by saying, "Who hath made man's mouth? Or who makes the dumb, or deaf, or the seeing, or the blind? Have not I, the LORD" (Ex. 4:11). God even offered Moses that he would "be with thy mouth, and teach thee what thou shalt say" (Ex. 4:12). When Moses persisted in taking Aaron, God relented. Moses possibly missed a healing miracle by clinging to his impediment rather than God's promise.

God made a concession to Moses' plea and allowed his brother Aaron to accompany him as his mouthpiece. Moses, even then, limited the power of God in his life by this act of mistrust. We must understand that God will especially use us in our points of weakness because it is there He will receive the most acknowledgment and glory, which is exactly what the world needs to see. When Moses did not trust God to provide for his communication deficit, he was allowed to take Aaron, who was often a hindrance rather than a blessing to Moses' ministry. It was Aaron who fashioned the golden calf, and who, along with their sister Miriam, spoke against Moses' wife. Later, it was Aaron along with Miriam who spoke against Moses' leadership causing God Himself to intervene. By failing to completely trust God, Moses created a situation that was to limit his effectiveness. Simply stated, he reaped what he sowed.

Moses' trust issues were very deep. In fact, he dealt with issues of trust throughout his life. Even so, God was able to use Moses in a phenomenal way. Although God does not wait for us to be perfect to use us, we must be willing to do his will.

Moses went though a lot of adversity in being perfected to be God's man. The forty years in the Midian wilderness, the trials and tests in dealing with Pharaoh, and the years of faithful service in leading the children of Israel through the desert to name a few.

Even though the adversity experience improved Moses' outlook, the issue of trust was a continuing issue in his experience. After all of the training that Moses received in the wilderness and all of the years of faithfulness leading Israel in the desert, he still did an act of faithlessness near the end of his life. Remember when God instructed Moses to speak to the rock when the Children of Israel needed water? When Moses smote the rock for water rather than speaking to it as he was instructed, it was as a result of the still not completely resolved childhood issue of trust. Many times the issues of our hearts are not completely settled even after a lifetime of God's leading. Thank God that He provides the grace to cover all of our shortcomings.

What gives me hope when I see my continuing weakness is that God did not just cast Moses away after his failure.

Justice would not allow Moses to lead the Children of Israel into the promise land after this very significant failing of smiting the Rock, a symbol of Christ. Grace and mercy interceded to not only allow Moses to see over into the promise land, some theologians believe that Moses was given a special resurrection after his death (See Jude 1:6). The gravity of Moses smiting the rock rather than speaking to it was that this Rock was an example of Christ being able to supply all of our needs. When Moses struck the Rock it was indicative of works rather than faith and without faith it is impossible to please God. Moses forfeited the right to lead the Children of Israel into the promise land because it was crucial that the crossing was epitomized by faith. When we sin, even out of the ignorance of our damaged heart and later discover the wrong of our actions, consequences still remain.

Although Moses was not allowed to lead the Children of Israel into the promise land, God more than rewarded him for his service. Not only was Moses allowed to see over into the land of promise, we must remember that in the special resurrection of Moses, he was afforded an honor that only one other human was to accomplish. It was the resurrected Moses, along with the chariot translated Elijah, who met with Christ on the mount of transfiguration. What a wonderful God we serve! Even in our weakness, God knows the true condition of our hearts. Though we might fail, He finds a way to reward us for the totality of our relationship. Moses is an example of all of those faithful who die and will take part in the first resurrection (See Rev. 20:6). Elijah is an example of all those faithful who will be alive at Christ's Second Coming and will be translated without experiencing death.

The story of the meek and mild Moses is an amazing illustration of God allowing adversity to heal the innermost issues of the heart of one who loved the Lord and was "called according to His purpose." The secular world does not understand the ways of God's Kingdom. In the world, to be outwardly strong and assertive is a quality to be admired and lauded. In the Kingdom of God, the tables are turned and to be meek means that we have been prepared to inhabit the earth at Christ's Second Coming, "For the meek shall inherit the earth."

God took the areas of mistrust causes by Moses' childhood "issues" and turned it toward the good of His work. As Moses dealt with the adversity that he faced, he was able to clearly see God's hand in every circumstance of his life. Unbeknown to Moses at the time, taking care of those sheep for forty years in the desert prepared him for the ministry of his life. One may wonder if just being in the desert some forty years qualifies as adversity? Consider what these years meant for Moses.

The first forty years of Moses life was spent in the public limelight being lauded for his greatness. Yet the middle forty years, the time when a man feels that he must make his mark, were spent in virtual obscurity. During these years, I would imagine that Moses felt that his ministry, which started out in a blaze of glory, would be relegated to the scrap heap of history. By the end of his sojourn in Midian, he was eighty years old.

Moses had been at the center of earthly greatness while in Pharaoh's Court. He was formerly a royal part of the greatest Kingdom on Earth. In fact, Moses was in the royal line of succession of Pharaoh, which meant he would have eventually been worshiped as God. The ancient Jewish historian Josephus wrote that Moses had been a great general at a very early age and was lauded as a military genius after he saved Egypt from the powerful Ethiopian army.

Imagine this well decorated soldier, in the line of succession to be the ruler of the most powerful kingdom on Earth, now tending dumb, stinky sheep. You had better believe that Moses' desert time qualifies as adversity. As he dealt with this situation, Moses had every reason to allow bitterness to overtake him. Yet during the obscurity of this forty-year sojourn in the Midian desert, Moses did not show bitterness and, as we view his life, we realize that he became better.

God needed a person of very special qualities for the daunting task of leading the Children of Israel out of Egyptian slavery. Although Moses fit the temporal requirements better than any man on earth, this leader needed something more: the heart and mind to intimately know God. God needed someone who was meek enough to allow himself to be led in all of his ways. After the adversity experiences of Moses' life, he perfectly fit this most important qualification. Moses is the perfect example of the Fourth Adversity Principle: *God allows adversity to teach Christians the lessons of trust.*

The Bible describes Moses as being more meek and humble than anyone on the face of the earth (See Numbers 12:3). The Bible is not an instrument of exaggeration, and the description of Moses as being meek is not hyperbole. God needed a person of extraordinary capabilities and Moses was that man. But the man was far different after his adversity experiences. While he had many of the temporal qualifications before his adversity experience, it was not until he experienced adversity that Moses was ready spiritually to be used for the task at hand. Moses was eventually used because his life experiences had shaped him into the meekness that was needed to fit into the plan of God. It is through our weakness that God's strength is made perfect (See II Cor. 12:9).

While we tend to look on externals, God is concerned that his leaders have internalized the qualities of His Kingdom. Conventional wisdom would not have put the quality of meekness as a requirement for the one who would fit this leadership profile. It is through our humbleness that God's power is made manifest in our lives and ministry. Moses was used of God after his "issues" had been resolved through the adversity principle.

Moses was reduced from an heir of the richest kingdom in the world to a lowly keeper of sheep, yet he was being prepared for greater service to the Master. Moses learned that his material possessions did not matter because as long as he was in the will of God he had true purpose.

We have no example of Moses claiming wealth or riches to indicate God's presence in his life. In fact, as you read the story of the 40-year sojourn of the Children of Israel in the wilderness, we see that Moses was a man who had put his life in the hands of the Master regardless of the sacrifice. After Moses had endured his adversity experience, he had died to self and the result was that God used him like no other. Moses was only focused on doing the will of God and he was used beyond measure.

Is it your purpose to be in the will of God, or are you focused on the things of this world? Are you claiming the overcoming experience of relationship, or are you claiming the things of this world? If you really want to be essential to God's plan, turn your focus from the things of this world. Then God will equip you to be used in this world and Kingdom to come. God intends to prosper the Christian, according to His purpose, not ours. Are you ready to be prospered in God's way? Lets look how that operates under Adversity Principle 5.

PRINCIPLE V: GOD ALLOWS ADVERSITY TO TEACH CHRISTIANS HIS AGAPE LOVE

CHAPTER 7
ADVERSITY AND MODERN PRESUMPTIONS

When we learn to experience the peace and security that results from the knowledge of God's love, the world becomes a radically different place. Satan continually attempts to obscure God's message of love in order to keep us from the best that the Master has to offer. The evil one's sophistry is particularly successful when he can blame God for the havoc that he, Satan, has caused. Adversity Principle Number 5 states that: *God allows adversity to teach Christians His Agape Love.*

To deceive us, Satan attempts to control the dominant presumptions that underlie our belief system. Secular presumptions serve to obscure God's love and purpose from the view of the unsaved multitudes. Unfortunately, many Christians also have presumptions that cloud their recognition of God's leading. Any belief system that is not ordered according to God's word will result in a perversion that will eventually deceive. To be within God's perfect plan for our lives we often have to let go of cherished thoughts, beliefs and sometimes, people.

When I was a child my older brother Paul was my companion, babysitter and often played the dual role of protector/detractor. Paul and I were inseparable.

One summer our father bought new fishing rods with the provision that we were to use the fishing rods only when he was with us. Of course the first chance we got we smuggled the fishing rods out of the house while Daddy was at work.

We took the new rods to a little fishing hole. To say the water was a fishing hole romanticizes the situation because it actually was a little pond of water that bordered the local dump. It was even called the backwater but, at our age, we just wanted to fish and the ambience mattered little. It was a very hot day and the smells from the dump were less than pleasing. Large dragonflies would flutter by and, every now and then, a rat would peak from under the trash, probably wondering what kind of foolish people would be fishing in this mess. Actually, Paul was the only one fishing and I made that more difficult because I was skipping rocks near where he was trying to catch fish.

On through the stifling hot morning he continued to cast his line into the murky waters. Suddenly, he caught something on his line. He excitedly called out to me as he started to reel in what he thought was the catch of the day. As he struggled with the line I stood afar off anxiously watching to see the triumph of my big brother using his new fishing pole. As he continued to reel in the catch our anticipation grew.

Just as he locked the reel and gave the line the final tug to reveal his catch, we both realized something was terribly wrong. Instead of seeing the expected glistening bass, catfish or even carp, my brother had caught ... a snake. I can remember shouting, "Snake!" Actually shouting was the last thing I can remember for a while because I started to run towards home. I looked back to see my big brother running right behind me. The only problem was that he still had the fishing pole in his hand and on the end of the pole the confused snake was still dangling as he ran. Paul continued to run and the snake continued to dangle.

Finally, after we ran for a while I shouted to him "Paul... drop the pole!" He refused because there was no way he was going to go home without the fishing pole that Dad had just bought that we were not supposed to be using anyway. While he ran with his pole the problem, the now totally exhausted snake, was just as close as it had always been. He could not hold on to the pole and rid himself of the problem.

We are often faced with the dilemma that my brother faced. We cannot rid ourselves of our presumptions unless we are willing to drop something that is valuable to us. As long as we hold on to the erroneous presumption the negative attachment remains. Many of the presumptions that the Christian community holds to are perverted presumptions that are limiting the influence of the Church in these last days.

A modern example of a perverted presumption that many Christians embrace is the aforementioned teaching of self-love that has infiltrated Christianity through the secular psychology movement. The question of whether we should love ourselves is usually answered according to secular psychology rather than from a reasonable, informed Biblical exegesis. The twentieth century witnessed a shift from the Biblical formation of love through submission to Christ, to an almost wholesale embrace of self-love that is antithetical to the Biblical admonition of "dying to self."

The even more recent perverted prosperity and abundance message, otherwise known as the health-and-wealth, name-it-and-claim-it teaching, also leads many believers into a set of false presumptions about God based on fleshly desires rather than spiritual need. The term "perverted prosperity" message is used to distinguish the modern doctrine from the authentic Biblical faith message. The authentic message of faith is an articulation of God's ability and willingness to provide for his children. This true faith message has increasingly been perverted into a doctrine that supports materialism and self-indulgence. The false doctrine affects the adherent's ability to see God's positive presence in the midst of negative circumstances.

Since God is love, His concern for us is immeasurable and thus it is His very nature to provide for our actual needs. The important question is, what are our actual needs? Whenever Christians complete a need assessment, we must be mindful to make our calculation from a paradigm that is foundationally different from the perspective of the secular world. Christians are pilgrims in this sin sick world and, since we are "in the world" but never to be "of the world", our view and response to need should be radically different from the world's. Hence, our presumptions must be based on God's word, rightly divided, which is often at odds with or considered foolishness by worldly standards.

For instance, we all share the same human needs: The physical needs of food, water, shelter and relative health, the mental need of information, challenge and relative soundness of mind, the social need of closeness and companionship with others, and the spiritual need of God conscientiousness. In our human effort to meet these needs, we prioritize what we consider to be the most essential needs of our lives. This approach lends itself to an emphasis on the things that we view as immediate need, food, water and shelter followed by the pursuit of mental acuity and the social need of companionship. Finally, if all our other needs are met and we have the time to consider it, we devote time to our spiritual need.

The problem with this type of needs assessment is that our most important needs are obscured by wants and shortsighted attempts to relieve what seems to be the immediate crisis. Conversely, God has a plan to meet all of our needs but His purpose has an eternal foundation and, if we allow Him control, He provides a perspective that will make us fully whole.

While our natural focus tends toward the immediate, God's omniscient view rightly focuses on eternal consequences. When Christ informs us to "seek ye first the Kingdom of heaven and its righteousness and all these things will be added", He is presenting the Father's perspective on meeting needs. We are to live in a present trust relationship with God and out of that relationship He will provide for all of our needs.

Therefore, God's perspective centers on our spiritual requirements that are actually more pressing than food, water or shelter, and ultimately more important than companionship with others. God knows that as we allow Him to meet our spiritual needs, the quality our lives will be enhanced in the now and for eternity, and all the things necessary for an uplifted, fulfilled life will be provided.

We too often spend an inordinate amount of time trying to figure out what our temporal needs are, and even more in trying to meet them. Our spiritual life, which is the true responsibility of our experience, is often not energetically cultivated. Our responsibility, we postulate, is to eschew evil and do good within our sphere, but in doing so we are often perplexed at our personal circumstances and the conditions of the world around us. Actually, our ultimate responsibility is to trust God and surrender to His will as we cultivate our spiritual experience.

A lack of understanding of why we find ourselves in negative circumstances can put us in the position of bewilderment. The natural desire for control will turn to discouragement as we realize that we cannot always control our negative situations. The temporal mind-set tends to persist in this state of discouragement and perplexity while attempting to figure things out. Conversely, the child of God, who has developed an eternal perspective, has the opportunity to live a life where discouragement is always overcome as we learn to view all circumstances through the eye of faith.

The key is to hear the voice of God in our lives, despite the extrinsic circumstances. Since God is all knowing, His way always provides the optimum solution. As we learn to trust Him for our circumstances and surrender to His will, God is able to bring us into His perfect will. When our vision is clouded by the temporal, we fail to see how simple the choice is; Either trust God for our circumstances through faith or fail to have faith and miss the preparation for the ultimate need of mankind, Eternal life.

We have the choice to develop faith and have the wonderful experience of eternal life, or allow doubt to control us that will cloud out faith and ultimately lead to darkness and death. God's process for preparing us for eternal life gives us a wonderful life experience as a portal to the eternity that actually starts now. God is ever endeavoring for us to hear His voice and follow Him as we release the cares of this world.

It is therefore important to identify and eliminate our false presumptions as we allow the messages of God's word to create in us the true basis for surrender. False presumptions lead Christians to embrace the voice of the world and its value system rather than the voice of God. These worldly values will lead to selfishness, which, uncorrected, will ultimately obscure the mission that we are called to perform. Conversely, God is pursuing us in order to perfect our characters, cultivate our love and generate in us an absolute trust in Him that will lead us to totally embrace His will for our lives.

Our trust must transcend the outward circumstances as we assimilate more fully into the Master's ultimate kingdom that is built on a foundation of love and trust. As we yield ourselves to the indwelling power of the Holy Spirit, the fruit of love, joy, and peace will be shown in our relationship with God. The fruit of patience, kindness and generosity will be shown to others and our lives will reveal faithfulness, gentleness and self control (temperance) (See Gal. 5:22-25). The fruit of the Spirit will allow us to embrace God's will for our lives.

Whenever we erroneously interpret the message of the Bible, we will develop false presumptions. For instance, some people mistakenly, and possibly unwittingly, accepted an unbalanced Biblical message that made poverty a virtue. This false presumption leaves many Christians with a dysfunctional approach to the creation and maintenance of wealth and personal financial responsibility. Instead of using wealth creation to bless others and the kingdom of God, this false presumption causes many to either refuse to use their abilities to create and manage wealth or fail to use their financial means to invest in the advancement of the kingdom. There is no Biblical foundation to consider poverty as a virtue. True virtue is established only by living within God's authority, whatever the circumstances.

The perverted prosperity movement has recently propelled the issue of wealth accumulation to the other extreme. In fact, many Christians now embrace a system of belief that overemphasizes the place and benefits of temporal wealth. The modern prosperity movement emphasizes material accumulation and equates it with God's approval. Many have now become so earthly prosperity minded that they are losing the longing for an eternal home where Christ's perfect order dwells, the wicked cease from troubling and the righteous find true rest. Instead, this modern presumption is enticing the Church to be content with earthly goals while failing to desire, plan for, and assist in the establishment of God's ultimate kingdom.

These teachings, along with other modern presumptions, have multitudes of Christians praying for riches and ease of life and embracing their inner selves as they claim material prosperity rather than spiritual renewal. Lost in this process is the Biblical revelation that God uses adversity, rather than ease, pleasure, and material abundance to cultivate character.

The fact that God allows adversity in order to mature His children does not mean that the Christian should live in fear, expect to live in poverty, or have any apprehension that tragedy or tribulation may be in the future. The truth is just the opposite. God intends for

Christians to live expectant, joyful, abundant and fearless lives. An understanding of the adversity principles allows informed Christians to live unburdened by *any* fear.

No matter what may befall us as children of the Triune God, we are assured that our Heavenly Father is trustworthy and we are to be secure in his care. Since we are in the caring, loving hand of the Master, the Christian should never become bitter because of circumstances. A clearer sensitivity to the Father's methods will empower us to better understand how God is in control of our circumstances and thus our trust in Him can be absolute. This sensitivity will also maximize our profits from the trials that God allows but never causes, and will empower us to grow closer to Him without the agony of mistrust. Simply stated, if we do not become bitter when adversity comes our way, we will become closer to God and thus better because of the experience.

Understanding how God utilizes adversity provides us with a better perspective as we deal with our personal situations as well as our observation of the suffering of the world. Through the eye of faith we must ever claim our Heavenly Father's plan of redemption from the travail that Satan brings.

God's work on behalf of our fallen world is twofold. First, He is universal Father to all because He is the Creator. Even those who do not recognize or acknowledge God as the Lord of their lives are still under His authority as Creator and are alive only because of His love and care. God strives to bring the fallen, unsaved world into a saving relationship with Him.

Second, to the trusting Christian, God is Abba, our intimate, available and loving Father. To all those who have accepted their heir ship through the saving redemption of Jesus Christ, God is not only Creator but also Redeemer. As Christians we have the distinct privilege of being in an intimate, saving relationship with the Father. When we are in this intimate relationship with God he is able to work out His perfect will for our lives.

For the ones who have not accepted the salvation of God through Jesus Christ, God's mission is to bring them to a saving knowledge of His grace. Adversity in the unredeemed life has a different function than the adversity that is allowed in a believer's experience. The Biblical examples of adversity in sinners' lives show us how God is always at work to provide ways for the sinner to be partakers of His grace.

The Christian is informed "all who would live Godly in Christ Jesus shall suffer persecution"(II Tim. 3:12). It is not a matter of if, but when we will deal with adversity. Even more importantly, it is not an issue of whether we will survive adversity, but how. We have the opportunity for adversity to improve our life experiences and Christian walk, if we will let go of our ungodly presumptions and allow God to have ruler ship over our lives. Oh, that we would learn the blessing of allowing God to have total control through surrender to His sovereign will. In this midst of adversity always remember the Fifth Adversity Principle: *God allows adversity to teach Christians His Agape Love.*

CHAPTER 8
DOES THE BIBLE INSTRUCT US TO LOVE OURSELVES ?

"And they overcame him by the blood of the Lamb, and by the word of their testimony; and they loved not their lives unto the death." Revelations 12:11

An important modern presumption that frustrates our ability to surrender our desire to have total sway in our own lives is the love of self. The modern self-love movement teaches that we cannot love others unless we first love ourselves. Contrarily, the Bible instructs us as Christians that we must die to ourselves. A review of the self-love theory reveals that this doctrine did not arise through accurate Biblical exegesis.

The modern psychology movement has legitimized the fallacy of self-love and modern Christianity has embraced this presumption that is in direct opposition to how God's kingdom was designed. Instead of self-love, we should internalize the Fifth Adversity Principle: *God allows adversity to teach Christians His Agape Love.*

At one time I too assented to the self-love principle. I had been in secular counseling for the panic disorder that I have already alluded to. Virtually all of the counseling sessions concentrated on or included elements of the need for self-love. I read many volumes of books on the subject and all seemed to be in agreement that the way to recovery for virtually any psychological disorder was to esteem and love oneself. While I was originally uneasy at the suggestions of the need to love myself, I found, to my surprise, that virtually all of the Christian authors on Psychology agreed with their secular counterparts. Although I did not realize it at the time, I have now come to the realization these sources had no valid scriptural authority to support the theory of self-love.

Since the counseling seemed to help me explore issues related to my past, I thought that maybe the self-love theory was right. I started to incorporate this self-love theory into my sermons and talks. I remember the first time that I was confronted with the dichotomy of self-love and what this movement meant to scriptural interpretation.

On this particular occasion, a sincere young man, stopped to compliment me on the presentation that included tenements of the need for-self love. He then added, with some hesitancy and absolutely no malice, that "the suggestion to love self does not seem to agree with the Biblical admonition that we should guard against ourselves and die to ourselves." While I was a little taken aback, not only at his forthrightness, but, even more importantly, at his sincerity, I decided to reexamine the topic in detail. Fully expecting to find volumes of information in the Bible and historical religious writings about the need to love oneself, I was utterly amazed at the lack of Biblical and theological basis for this concept.

The Bible texts used to support the view of self-love, primarily center upon the command to love our neighbors as ourselves as found in both the Old and New Testaments. The most often used of these texts is Christ's recitation of the law of love. When asked, "Teacher, which is the great commandment in the law", Christ responded "Thou shalt Love the lord thy God with all thy heart, and with all thy soul, and with all thy mind. This is the first and great commandment." Christ continued by adding that "the second is like unto it, Thou shalt love thy neighbor as thyself. Upon these two," Christ explained, "hang all the Law and Prophets" (Matt: 22: 36-40). Could anyone argue with the fact that Christ was commanding us to love ourselves as we love our neighbor? The command was that we should love ourselves, or was it?

In answer to this question, I strongly urge you to consider a book by Dr. Paul Brownback, entitled *The Danger of Self-Love: Re-Examining a Popular Myth*[3]. Brownback considers this question in full detail and with a layperson appropriate exegesis of the scriptural context. This author makes a full examination of the Biblical

---

[3] Paul Brownback, *The Danger of Self-Love*. Chicago: Moody Press, 1982.

evidence and arrives at the conclusion that we are not commanded to love ourselves as the modern teaching advises. Dr. Brownback quotes Jay Adams, another author who challenges the self-love theory, and effectively counters the idea that Christ was commanding us to love ourselves:

> When Christ said that the whole law could be summed up in two commandments (love for God and love for one's neighbor), He intended to say exactly that and nothing else. Yet some Christians (with a psychologizing bent) and some psychiatrists who are Christians are not satisfied with that; they (dangerously) add a third commandment: love yourself.
>
> ...the fact that Christ distinguished but "two commandments" (vs. 40) is decisive. Had He intended to stress a third (particularly when one of the other two was dependent upon it) He could not have done so by using the language He employs in this passage. Such psychologizing of the passage erases its plain intent and seriously diverts its stress...It is incorrect and dangerous, therefore, to make a large point out of that about which Christ did not make a point at all (and indeed, which He explicitly excluded by the limiting word *two*).[4]

There is no effective counter either in the popular literature or, most importantly, in the Bible, to Jay Adams' proposition that Christ was not commanding us to love ourselves in this passage. As Brownback also cogently points out, if Christ had wanted to command people to love themselves, a third clear directive would seem to be needed, especially if a lack of self-love is a major problem, as the current counseling technique asserts. The reason that Christ did not give a third command in this passage was because he was not commanding us into a proposition of self-love, he was stating a principle of love toward God and our fellow man.

The parallel teaching to the Matthew proposition is found in Luke 10: 25-37, where Christ used the story of the "Good Samaritan" to illustrate this point. Christ's use of the story of the person who went

---

[4] Ibid. p. 51.

out of his way to show love for his neighbor is indicative of what loving your neighbor as yourself means. Simply put, love in this context is action, not statements or even feelings of affection. Love, in the story of the Good Samaritan, is characterized by the willingness to act, "to interrupt your schedule, and use up your oil, wine, and money to achieve what you think is best for your neighbor."[5] The reason that Christ commands us to love our neighbor as ourselves is because he was instructing us that what we want for ourselves we should desire for our neighbor. The same natural inclination we have to meet our own needs, to feed ourselves and find shelter should be utilized in our love for our neighbor. As Dr. Brownback explains:

> [T]he inclination to meet our own needs, to feed ourselves and find shelter - is part of our human make-up. Normally it takes no urging to motivate a person to care for himself. On the contrary, it usually requires restraint to stop such satisfaction of need. Jesus says that a person should do likewise for his neighbor, and in other places, for a stranger or even an enemy. No one needs to *command* me to meet my own needs; that response is built in. But when it comes to meeting my neighbor's needs, I have not been wired by nature to be automatically sensitive to his concerns. So Christ's command calls me to that kind of awareness.[6]

No, Christ was not giving us a new command to be affectionate toward ourselves, he was commanding us to have the same type of outward action for others as we do inward motivations to take care of our own needs. We are to love our neighbors and desire for them the same type of things that we would naturally desire for ourselves.

Paul picks up on this principle when he instructs husbands to "love their wives as their own bodies. He that loves his wife loves himself" (Eph. 5:28). The instruction is not to have a sentimental

---

[5] Piper, John. *Is Self-Love Biblical?* Christianity Today, 12 August 1977, pp. 6-9, as quoted in Paul Brownback, *The Danger of Self-Love*. Chicago: Moody Press, 1982.

[6] Brownback, *The Danger of Self-Love*. 59-60.

love for ourselves, it is a directive to husbands that by taking care of their wives they are taking care of themselves because the two are "twain one flesh". Paul is not teaching self-love as the self-love theorists have suggested, he is teaching husbands that the same rationale for a natural self-preservation should be extended to the wife because they are one.

Importantly, it is also Paul who alerts us, in unequivocal terms, to the danger of self-love. In a letter that speaks to this issue and to our time like no other, Paul warns that one of the signs of the last age will be that society will be inundated by the theory of self-love that has become a dominant presumption of our age. Unfortunately, the Christian community seems to disregard the importance of his warning! Consider this admonition in the light of the modern self-love theory:

> This know also, that in the last days perilous times shall come. For men shall be ***lovers of their own selves*** covetous, boasters, proud, blasphemers, disobedient to parents, unthankful, unholy, without natural affection, truce breakers, false accusers, incontinent, fierce, despisers of those that are good, traitors, heady, high minded, lovers of pleasures more than lovers of God; ***Having a form of godliness***, but denying the power thereof; from such turn away. (Bold and italics added by author) (II Tim.3:1-5)

Paul is warning us, in no uncertain terms, that one of the most important and notable signs of the last days will be when the world is gripped by people being lovers of their own selves. The fact that the self-love theory originated in secular society and has been given a religious facade is very important.

The worldly tenements of self-love, which started in the secular psychology movement, have now invaded all segments of society including the Church. In this text, Paul anticipates this infiltration and unholy alliance. Paul first emphasizes that one of the signs of the perilous last days will be that men will be lovers of themselves with all of the attendant ills. He then ends the passage by indicating that the adherents to this doctrine will have a "form of godliness" but this form will be denied power. He then commands us to turn away from those who are like this, and by implication, those who teach this "other" gospel. It is time for the Church to turn away from this false gospel.

The effect of self-love is crucial for us to consider as we examine the principles of adversity. One reason that we are instructed to turn away from such teachings is because it will ill equip the Church for the faith that is needed to stand for truth. When we accept the dominant presumption that we should love ourselves, we will not be willing to make the sacrifice necessary to be used of God in these perilous last days.

As I observe the different television ministries that advocate the self-love theory as well as the perverted prosperity message, I am impressed that we are seeing a "form of godliness" and that these doctrines are becoming increasingly accepted without qualification. It seems that there is a new twist to these presentations every week. This observation makes the rest of Paul's admonition even more important in that adherents to this false message will be: Ever learning, and never able to come to the knowledge of the truth. Now as Jannes and Jambres withstood Moses, so do these also resist the truth; men of corrupt minds, reprobate concerning the faith (II Tim.3:7-8).

As I consider this portion of Paul's teaching, I am overwhelmed with the magnitude of the damage that the false teaching of self-love is achieving within the Christian community. I hang my head in deep contrition that the purity of the gospel is being perverted as we have these great movements that are deceiving God's people and keeping the adherents from growing in the grace that adversity affords. These modern presumptions have so invaded the Church that to question their origins seem sacrilegious. The self-love movement is opening the door for a myriad of inappropriate teachings.

Importantly, Paul compares this situation to that of Jannes and Jambres, who withstood Moses. Jannes and Jambres were the magicians in Pharaoh's Courts who met the miracles sent from God through Moses, with a counterfeit. Remember when Moses had Aaron cast his rod before Pharaoh? The rod then turned into a serpent as a sign from God. In response these court magicians were able to counterfeit the act by having their rods also turn to serpents. Aaron's rod then swallowed up the counterfeit of Jannes and Jambres

(See Exodus 7:10-12). I believe that the counterfeit message of self-love will eventually be swallowed up by the principles of God's truth, but many will be deceived, some to their eternal ruin. Many others will be inhibited in their end time ministry by accepting the false presumptions of our age.

Paul then says that these teachers were men of corrupt minds and reprobate concerning the faith. The Greek word that Paul uses for corrupt is "kataphtheiro," which means to spoil entirely. The corruption of the self-love movement goes to the core of the Gospel message and affects every other doctrine of the Church. This premise is foundational, and all other facets of the adherent's life will be compromised.

In addition, Paul says that these teachers will be "reprobate" concerning the faith, which basically means worthless. These modern teachings are so dangerous because they do not equip us for eternity. The strategies, which accompany the doctrines of self-love and prosperity, are pleasing for the moment, but are eventually fruitless because they fail to equip its adherent's for participation in God's eternal kingdom that is built on selflessness and the actualized acceptance of God.

The reaction to the teaching of self-love is telling. I was at a prominent local church when an attractive, articulate and cheerful young female high school student was delivering the morning announcements. After the announcements, she gave a list of what she thought it takes to be successful. After a litany of interesting and appropriate admonitions, she ended by saying "most importantly, we should love ourselves first and most." This last word of advice was met with a chorus of agreement. As I witnessed this exchange, I thought of the almost total societal devotion to the tenets of self-love.

I was discussing this issue with a Christian acquaintance who has been in counseling for a psychological disorder. Interestingly, she has dealt with some of the same secular and Christian counselors that I have and, in addition, she also has some graduate training in secular counseling. She was taken aback at the suggestion that the Bible does not teach self-love. When I asked her to support this proposition through the Bible, she was unable to, but then with great sympathy she said, "Well I know your family background and I think that it is so sad that you do not love yourself." She was sincere and I don't mean this as a criticism, but this false doctrine is so pervasive that many well-meaning Christians refuse to even consider its origin.

This false doctrine is so accepted that to identify its lack of Biblical foundation causes many to find other non-Biblical support when the presumption is challenged. As we grapple with psychological issues, the doctrine of self-love is indicative of a profound spiritual counterfeit.

I do not believe that the doctrine of self-love will provide for the real meaningful change needed for the Christian, but it can provide some immediate relief for those who have psychological issues. The problem with a counterfeit is that it is very close to the real and, for a time, may even provide a semblance of a solution. But we are to look for a lasting solution borne out of a relationship with Christ and His word, not a quick fix to help us in the immediate situation. A short review of a theological precept is important as we deal with the difference between the lasting solution of God, as revealed in the Scripture, and the quick fix of the self-love proponents in dealing with our psychological difficulties. Lets briefly examine God's way of dealing with our psychological issues for the long term.

When a person comes to a saving knowledge of Christ we are immediately forgiven and seen by the Father as if we had never sinned; this is justification. We can have assurance that we are justified through the merits of Jesus Christ which means we are saved.

Although we are immediately justified and viewed by the Father as if we had never sinned, the legacy and predisposition of our sinfulness must be put off of our mortal bodies. After we have repented and confessed our sins, we then start the Christian journey. This journey is comprised of being covered and justified by the merits of Christ. The journey also includes our becoming "like" Christ, as we die to self and allow Christ to live in us through this process known as sanctification. Sanctification is the work of the Holy Spirit, which last throughout our lives. In this process of becoming like Christ, God is leading and molding the Christian as we yield our lives on a daily basis. Sanctification is Christ in us, the hope of glory.

The Church has done a very good job in disseminating to its adherents the good news of justification, and with good reason. What a wonderful God we have, that takes us in our sinful state and provides a way for us "while we were yet sinners." The mystery of how God is able to take fallen man and provide salvation, through the merits of His son, Jesus Christ, is the most amazing revelation of all times. The mere thought of how good God is to provide a way of escape for the sinner is enough to make me to stop and proclaim my love and devotion to our Lord and Savior, Jesus Christ. Glory to the precious Holy Name of Christ who takes away my sins.

God would have still been righteous had he destroyed mankind when we disobeyed, but in his goodness and mercy, he devised a way to put man in a position as if he had never sinned. "There is therefore now no condemnation to them which are in Christ" (Romans 8:1). This is the good news of justification.

But there is another, often misunderstood part of the amazing good news of salvation that God provides through Christ Jesus. The church has often failed to spread the rest of the good news of salvation, namely, the *good life*. We are not only justified before a Holy God, He has promised us power to live faithful, overcoming lives. This is the process of sanctification. This power of sanctification must be utilized in the life of a believer in order for us to receive the full healing power of God. This is the discipline of grace.[7]

God's grace allows us to be changed into the similitude of Jesus Christ. This change takes time as God takes our sinful nature and molds us and makes us after His will. Many times we think that a lifetime of living in the flesh will be changed overnight. But God works in us skillfully and patiently on a daily basis. He takes the innermost issues of our hearts and exposes them to His grace. During this time our flesh will look for immediate, quick and easy answers and, if we are not well grounded in the Scriptures, we will look to fleshly means to speed up the process. This is a set up for deception. That is why we must ever examine our methods and conclusions to make sure that they are biblically based.

If we are not grounded in Scriptures, even those who have given

---

[7] I highly recommend a most excellent work on this topic by Jerry Bridges from which I have gleaned this term. Jerry Bridges, *The Discipline of Grace*. Colorado Springs, CO: Navpress 1994.

their hearts to the Lord will be susceptible to deception. What sounds good is not necessarily right, and all things must be accepted or rejected under the perfect light of God's Holy Word. To avoid deception and live within the discipline of God's grace, which will ultimately heal all of the issues of our hearts, there are certain principles that are crucial to the Christian experience of sanctification. To paraphrase Jerry Bridges' suggestions on the discipline of grace, we must:

1. Have a through knowledge of God's word. We must start by knowing what God's word has to say in order to have a frame of reference to combat deception. Bible memorization should be a part of every Christian's study life.

2. We must meditate on God's word in order to internalize the word's meaning in our lives. Meditation of God's word will take us from a cursory knowledge of the word and, as we meditate of the word of God, I believe that God, through the Holy Spirit, will give us a deep knowledge that is beyond human understanding,

3. We must apply the Scriptures to concrete situations in our daily lives, which will allow us to develop biblically based convictions. We must acknowledge the word of God in all of the situations of our lives, and weigh all information that we receive by the light of God's word.

4. As we develop Bible based convictions, we are transformed by the Holy Spirit more and more into the likeness of Christ.

Thank God for this power of grace in the Christian's life. God's word teaches us in many different ways how the power of grace leads us into victory in all of the areas of our lives. Paul succinctly informs us :"For the grace of that brings salvation has appeared to all men. It teaches us to say "no" to ungodliness and worldly passions, and to live self-controlled, upright and godly lives in this present age" (Titus 2:11-12. (NIV)).

God is in the process of healing the Christian's heart. The evidence of the healing is increasingly apparent as we become more like Christ. This is called the process of sanctification. This is no quick fix. God uses various means to heal the psychological weaknesses found in the Christian's heart. The self-love approach to these psychological weaknesses, which are actually the enduring vestiges of our sin nature, is to advise the adherents to focus on their own needs and take care of their own selves. This approach often has short-term success because many people have issues related to abuse and neglect that makes them susceptible to mistrust and self-loathing. The self-love approach provides some relief because the adherents begin to perceive that they have worth.

The Bible reveals an even higher level of healing and self worth when we understand that we do not have to take care of ourselves. It is God who takes care of us in all of the issues of life as we seek His will. God provides the needed solutions and, as we embrace His primacy in our lives, He provides the peace that passes all understanding as He heals the issues of our hearts in real and tangible ways. Christ is not trying to give us a quick fix relief, He is endeavoring to bring us into the victorious relationship that is needed for an ultimate experience with our Creator and Redeemer.

Many Christians, under the deception of these modern presumptions, are failing to comprehend God's methods for true spiritual and psychological growth. While the flesh desires an immediate experience based upon our strengths, God deals with us in the areas of our mistrust and weakness so we are thoroughly prepared for His service. Author Don Mazat, a man who has done extensive research into the self-love movements speaks to this point:

> Most Christians today do not realize how important weakness, failure, discouragement, disappointment, suffering, testing, and trials are in the development of their Christian life. Through these dealings of God our natural sinful pride is being dealt with. God calls us away from ourselves in that through burying, rejecting, and denying self we may turn in faith unto our Lord Jesus and experience his life, peace, joy, and power. The apostle Paul wrote, 'I will boast all the more gladly about my weaknesses, so that Christ's power may rest on me' (2 Cor. 12:9).[8]

---

[8] Mazat, Don. *Christ-Esteem.* Eugene, Oregon: Harvest House, 1990. p. 79.

BITTER OR BETTER: THE ADVERSITY PRINCIPLES

As we appropriately deal with the issues that adversity reveals, we learn the true principles of being in God's service that will sustain us in our everyday lives and prepare us for the end of the age. Rather than loving the things of this world and ourselves in selfishness, we shall be overcomers. When we love ourselves, we are not overcoming Satan's demand on our lives. We should always consider Adversity Principle Number 5; *God allows adversity to teach us His agape love*. We need the following testimony of overcoming adversity:

> And I heard a loud voice saying in heaven, Now is come salvation, and strength, and the Kingdom of our God, and the power of his Christ; for the accuser of our brethren is cast down, which accused them before our God day and night.
>
> And they overcame him by the blood of the Lamb; and by the word of their testimony; ***and they loved not their lives unto death.*** (Rev.12:10-11 (Italics and bold added))

God does not command us to love ourselves, he commands Christians to die to ourselves, so that Christ may live in and through us. Our testimony will be of Christ and how he has brought us through. Even if it causes us tribulation and persecution we will not love our lives, even unto death. As the defects in our characters are made manifest by adversity, we will more clearly see the leading of God in our lives. We overcome adversary by the blood of the Lamb and by our testimony. Our testimony is how God has been with us in all of the issues of our lives. Do you have a testimony as to how God brought you through? If not, get ready, for God will do something special in your life so that you too will have a testimony of overcoming. Remember Adversity Principle Number 5: *God allows adversity to teach Christians His agape love.*

PRINCIPLE VI: GOD ALLOWS ADVERSITY TO GIVE CHRISTIANS THE PROPER PERSPECTIVE OF THIS WORLD AND THE WORLD TO COME

CHAPTER 9
PAUL AND THE PROSPERITY OF THE GOSPEL

"Not that I speak in respect of want: for I have learned, in whatsoever am, therewith to be content." Philistines 4: 11

The life of a Tarsus Jew named Saul is one of the most amazing stories found within the pages of the Scriptures. Saul, who was later known as Paul after his conversion to Christianity, had a distinguished life even before he started on his pivotal Christian journey. Paul's life is an example of the Adversity Principle Number 6: *God allows adversity to give Christians the proper perspective of this world and the world to come.*

When challenged about his credentials, Saul was able to recite a litany of all of the "right stuff." In his own words, he was circumcised on the eighth day according to the law, of the stock of Israel, of the tribe of Benjamin. A Hebrew of Hebrews and, as in regard to his position concerning the law, he was a Pharisee. He was a zealous advocate of the highest order and ordered his life according to all of the Moral, Ceremonial and Civil Laws (See Phil.3).

Paul was multilingual and held dual Israeli and Roman citizenship. In addition to his racial and religious pedigree, he was an extremely educated man. Paul was not only a general student of Israel's ruling body, the Sanhedrin, he was also a personal pupil of the highly respected Gamaliel. Gamaliel was an esteemed member of the Sanhedrin, a scholar of renown, held the title of Doctor of the Law and had a reputation known among all of the people (See Acts 5:34, 22: 3). In light of this background, it would not be a stretch to believe that Saul was not only a man of high social standing, he probably was a man of some material substance. In addition, Saul was a person who fit very well into the dominant culture of his time. From all extrinsic circumstances, materially as well as socially, Paul seemed to have no need of change in his life because he was a member of the elite. I offer this short background of Saul only to show his significance before his conversion to Christianity.

It is a well-known story how Saul, under the authority of the Sanhedrin, was involved in systematically persecuting the Church and the early Christians who were in Jerusalem immediately following the resurrection and ascension of Christ. In fact, when Stephen, the first martyr of the Church age, was stoned to death, it was Saul who consented to his death, and even held the coats of those who participated in the execution. After the stoning, Saul set out on a course of wreaking havoc on the early church. Saul would go door to door in order to identify Christians, after which he would take these men and women of faith to prison. Saul was a major threat to the viability of the early Church (See Acts 8, 9).

But then, one fortuitous day, in the midst of apparent societal acceptance and material abundance, Saul was on his way to Damascus. He was going there to in order to find whether there were any Christians that needed to be bound and brought to Jerusalem. On this dusty road Saul had a visitation from the resurrected Jesus Christ, and his life immediately changed from persecutor to follower of Christ, and servant to those he had been persecuting.

Saul was met with a light from heaven on his way to Damascus that caused him to fall to the earth. The voice said "Saul, Saul why persecutest thou me?" When Saul answered by saying "Who art thou Lord?" he received the significant response, "I am Jesus whom thou persecutes, it is hard for thee to kick against the pricks." Paul's response was immediate and decisive; "What wilt thou have me do" (See Acts 9:1-6).

And thus we see in a short magnificent moment, a dramatic change from the man named Saul who identified himself with establishment and persecuted the Church, to the man named Paul who probably did more than any other to establish God's Church. The change from Saul to Paul was facilitated through a personal relationship with Jesus Christ. Paul's change was so complete that from his conversion forward the only subject that interested this former Jewish zealot was the will of the Father through Jesus Christ. Paul could twice claim promise to all of the supposed blessings of prosperity, he was a child of Israel through Benjamin and he was a part of the kingdom of God through his relationship with and special calling from Jesus Christ, the Son of God.

If God intended for all of his people to be wealthy and prosperous in the things of this world, Paul would be the prime example. Instead of a life of ease, pleasure, and material prosperity, Paul's amazing and dedicated ministry was filled with persecutions, often accompanied by material needs and continual adversity. Where was the so-called prosperity message in the life of Paul?

When I see the various national ministeries claiming that the mark of God's blessing is material prosperity, I cannot help but to compare this modern false doctrine to the sacrificial life of Paul. In contrast to the modern boast of material prosperity that many in the church are teaching, consider Paul's own testimony of his life:

> Since many are boasting in the way the world does, I too will
> boast. You gladly put up with fools since you are so wise! In fact, you even put up with anyone who enslaves you or exploits you or takes advantage of you or pushes himself forward or slaps you in the face. To my shame I admit that we were too weak for that! What anyone else dares to boast about - I am speaking as a fool - I also dare to boast about. Are they Hebrews? So am I. Are they Israelites? So am I. Are they servants of Christ? (I am out of my mind to talk like this.) I am more.
>
> I have worked much harder, been in prison more frequently, been flogged more severely, and have been exposed to death again and again. Five times I received from the Jews the forty lashes minus one. Three times I was beaten

with rods, once I was stoned, three times I was shipwrecked, I spent a night and a day in the open sea, I have been constantly on the move. I have been in danger from my own countrymen, in danger from Gentiles, in danger in the city, in danger in the country, in danger at sea, in danger from false brothers. I have labored and toiled and have often gone without sleep; I have known hunger and thirst and have often gone without food; I have been cold and naked. Besides everything else, I face daily the pressure of my concern for all the churches. Who is weak, and I do not feel weak? Who is led into sin, and I do not inwardly burn?

If I must boast, I will boast of the things that show my weakness. The God and Father of my Lord Jesus, who is to be praised forever, knows that I am not lying. (II Cor.11:18-30 (NIV))

When I compare the testimony and life of Paul to the health/wealth, name it/claim it prosperity apostasy that is circulating in the modern churches, I am overwhelmed at the magnitude of the deception that is being established in this latter day. Paul knew nothing of this doctrine that all of God's people are to always be wealthy and healthy. Why didn't Paul name and claim his way out of trouble and destitution? Because he understood that the Kingdom of God was not of this world. He did not boast of houses and lands, he boasted of the adversity principle, because in his adversity he saw the hand of God on his life and ministry.

Paul often found himself in actual physical and material need. He had often been beaten with many stripes. Paul was also often hungry and thirsty with substantial periods without adequate food supplies and, in the midst of his ministry, he even had periods without adequate sleep. Paul was consistently in danger from virtually every corner. Shipwrecked, beaten with rods, stoned, and even a night and a day spent in the open sea, constituted only a part of the adversity that Paul faced.

In addition, Paul faced many other dangers. Danger from bandits, danger from his own countrymen, danger from Gentiles, danger in the city, danger in the country, danger at sea, and danger from false brethren. It would seem that Paul could have lamented how much better off he was before his conversion to Christianity, yet he never complained and stayed steadfast in his focus to do the will of God. Instead of being rich in the things of this world, Paul was content to be rich in the things of his ministry, rich in service. Paul's response to adversity is best illustrated in the following passage:

> "Not that I speak in respect of want: for I have learned, in whatsoever state I am, therewith to be content. I know both how to be abased, and I know how to abound: every where and in all things I am instructed both to be full and to be hungry, both to abound and to suffer need. I can do all things through Christ who strengthens me." (Phil. 4: 11-13)

Paul embraced a precept that is increasingly lost in the cacophony of modern fleshly presumptions. He understood that we are to store up spiritual treasures in heaven rather than embracing ease and temporal prosperity in the flesh. Our approach to the things of this world should be one of contentment with the understanding that we can do all things if we are in Christ. Christ strengthens us to endure whatever is necessary for the sake of the gospel. While there is no virtue in being poor, the goal is to do God's will in whatever state we find ourselves. When we are blessed with material things, we should thank God, share what we have and refuse to be caught up in the things that we have. When we suffer lack, we should thank God, ask for what we need and trust God for the outcome. We should find our contentment in being within God's will.

Paul well understood and lived the Sixth Principle of Adversity: *God allows adversity to give Christians the proper perspective of this world and the world to come.* We are given a view of Paul's understanding of the Sixth Principle as he reflects upon his life as he occupied a cell on death row. Paul, not long before he was to face the executioner's block and in his last admonition to the young minister Timothy, emphatically informed him of what is important for the Christian:

> I have fought a good fight, I have finished my course, I have kept the faith. Henceforth there is laid up for me a

crown of righteousness, which the Lord, the righteous judge, shall give me at that day: and not to me only, but unto all them that love his appearing.... For Demas hath forsaken me, having loved this present world and is departed unto Thessalonica. (II Tim. 4:7-8, 10 (first clause))

We should be endeavoring to secure crowns of righteousness not crowns of riches. When our view is obscured by an inappropriate concentration on the things of this world, we will fail to focus on the ultimate goal of God's will on earth and the ministry that is needed to lead sinners to God's heavenly kingdom. We, like Paul, must never allow anything to limit our concentration on the imminent coming of Jesus Christ, and the establishment of His everlasting kingdom. The crown of righteousness is for all those who "love His appearing."

A view of what happens to us when we focus of the things of this world is presented to us in this passage by the reference to Demas. Demas was a Christian and an associate who, in the midst of their ministry, forsook Paul. The reason that Demas did not endure in the ministry was, as Paul put it, because he loved this present world. We must each ask ourselves, are we falling into the trap that defeated Demas; friendship with the world culminating in the love of the things of this world? This is a chilling question that each Christian must squarely face.

Importantly, in the introduction to this same passage, Paul warns Timothy that he must always "preach the word," and that he should "rebuke (and) exhort with all longsuffering and doctrine." In an admonition that seems to be directed at many of the modern presumptions, and those who teach them, Paul warns:

> For the time will come when they will not endure sound doctrine; but after their own lusts shall they heap to themselves teachers, having itching ears; And they shall turn away their ears from the truth, and shall be turned into fables. (II Tim. 4: 3-4)

The time that Paul spoke of almost two thousand years ago is presenting itself in this modern age. Look and see for yourselves the excesses that are going on within the Church. We have national ministries that are admonishing congregations to visualize a lever that they pull as they chant absurdities such as "money is coming... now ...to me." Can you imagine Paul admonishing young Timothy to focus so much on ridiculous exercises of the control of mammon?

The time of material excess and spiritual delusion has come to the Church. The question that we should be centering on as Christians, is not how much money can we make, but how we can best deliver the purity of God's world to a sinful and perverse generation? How many of these ministries are teaching their followers how we should respond to adversity? Since we are being prepared for our ministry through adversity, this question is crucial. Are you ready to be used and improved through adversity?

CHAPTER 10
HOW GOD INTENDS TO PROPER CHRISTIANS

"Beloved, I wish above all things that thou mayest prosper and be in health, even as thy soul prospereth." III John 1:2

The perverted prosperity message is one of the most difficult of all of the modern presumptions to discuss and rebut. The teaching that God has promised that all believers should expect to acquire earthly health, wealth, and material abundance has become so blatant that many prosperity ministries unabashedly teach that God endeavors to make all of the adherents of the message "rich". People who have not attained material wealth are said to suffer from a poverty mentality. As ridiculous as some of the tenements of the message are, it can still be a difficult message to rebut. Importantly, this false presumption can serve to obscure the Adversity Principle Number 6: *God allows adversity to give Christians the proper perspective of this world and the world to Come*. One reason that it is so difficult to distinguish the true from the perverted message regarding prosperity is because there is much truth mingled with error in the prosperity movement.

There are abundant texts used to support the contentions of the prosperity movement, and, in truth, God has often used the blessing of material prosperity in dealing with His people. Some of the prosperity teaching reforms such as the espousal of stewardship and personal financial responsibility, the reduction of debt and the need for hard work and planning was needed within the body of Christ. Unfortunately, the prosperity message has taken a turn that is indicative of the last days in time. The teaching has been unwittingly used to promote worldliness, materialism and the encouragement of self within the body of Christ.

Within my lifetime, I have observed the perverted prosperity message emerge from the periphery of Christendom as epitomized by the flamboyant "Rev. Ike". A minister by the name of Frederick Eikernkoetter used to proclaim that God was in the business of making all of his adherent's rich and that it was perfectly acceptable to live ostentatiously. Rev. Ike used to say with a sly smile, "If you don't want your money, just send it to me." At one time these tenements were considered humorous and the message was relegated to the fringes of Christianity. This same prosperity message has now achieved mainstream acceptance and many mainline conservative denominations, the more liberal churches and charismatic fellowships have either a wholesale acceptance of the tenets of this doctrine or a variation of the underlying premise. It seems that there is a new ministry each week that rises to proclaim, in a most public way, that God wants Christians to be rich.

The end result is that the Church of the living God has become more earthly directed and materialistic than any time since the excesses of the middle ages. An example of middle age excess is when indulgences were sold to save people from purgatory. Purgatory was an extra-biblical doctrine. The doctrine taught that when a person died they went to a place for cleansing until they were fit for heaven. These indulgences were sold in order to allow a person to buy themselves or their loved one out of this unhappy place and gain them entrance into heaven. Of course, this was accomplished at a price, which also happened to fill the coffers of the Church and enrich the priests. This false doctrine did immeasurable damage to the cause of Christ during its time.

Now, at the close of Earth's history, is a time when the hearts of Christians need to be prepared for the proclamation of the end time gospel. Instead, the condition of the Church is more equipped to be involved in propping up the stock market than preparing the world for the times of trouble which will precede Christ's second coming. The false prosperity message has provided a moral underpinning for selfishness.

Jim Baker, the former televangelist, was one of the leading proponents of the prosperity gospel. In an adversity experience that is Job like in its magnitude, Baker lost everything and was sent to prison. Once in prison Baker made an exhaustive review of his mistakes, including his advocacy of the prosperity message. He has now humbly repudiated this false doctrine of materialism that has almost thoroughly pervaded the modern Church.[9] While in prison, Mr. Baker extensively reviewed the Scriptures that are used to promote the perverted prosperity message and came to the following conclusion:

> The more I studied the Bible, the more I had to face the awful truth: I had been teaching false doctrine for years and hadn't even known it. Tragically, too late, I recognized that at PTL I had done just the opposite of Jesus' words by teaching people to fall in love with money. Jesus never equated His blessing with material things, but I had. I laid so much emphasis upon materialism, I subtly encouraged people to put their hearts into things, rather than into Jesus. I should have taught them to fall in love with Jesus. He is the only One who will never leave us or forsake us when the money and possessions are gone.
>
> When I realized the truth, I was deeply grieved and repented over my error. How could I have been so wrong? How could I have missed Christ's true message so completely? His statements about material possessions in general, and money in particular, were clear. How could I have had the audacity to twist Jesus'

---

[9] I highly recommend Jim Baker's significant autobiography, *I was Wrong* (Nashville, Tenn.: Thomas Nelson, Inc. Publishers, 1996) which, in great detail, explains the deception of the prosperity movement. In addition, Baker's subsequent book, entitled *Prosperity and the Coming Apocalypse* (Nashville, Tenn.: Thomas Nelson Inc., Publishers, 1998), denounces the prosperity movement and explains the dangers of materialism in great detail. While I do not endorse all of Mr. Baker's views on end time events, his books are some of the most well written documentation of the dangers of the prosperity gospel.

statement into the opposite of what He had taught? [10]

The reason that Baker could have so easily taught the perverted prosperity message is because it is a doctrine that is amendable to the flesh, which is always easy to accept. Not only is this doctrine of the flesh easy to accept; it is natural. This is tragic because the world needs to have the Church represent the spiritual, not the natural. While some may argue that Baker was on the extreme of the prosperity movement, a cursory examination of recent prosperity trends, reveal that his teachings would be considered mainstream, if not somewhat conservative, by today's standard.

Much like the modern self-love movement, the modern prosperity movement has roots and many allies within secular society. While historic Christianity has always had a positive tension with forms of material excess, a review of the Church in apostasy reveals that whenever the Church was reflecting worldliness, an accommodation to materialism was established. We are currently in a time of unprecedented secular prosperity and expansion. There are now more millionaires being created each day than at any time in history, while much of the world remains in abject poverty. Western society is in need of a moral underpinning and excuse for this expansion and the resulting excess of lifestyle, and much of the Church has not only accommodated the excess, it has surpassed the world in ostentatious living.

A walk through a secular bookstore reveals titles that reflect the world's preoccupation with materialism and earthly riches. Books on the lifestyles of the rich and famous as well as "how to" books on becoming a millionaire abound. Recent television shows also reflect the secular concentration of wealth with shows enticing us to become worldly minded through all types of schemes as shown on a myriad of infomercials and network game shows which promise the chance to become an instant millionaire.

Sadly, the same messages are being promoted in Christian bookstores and Christian television. Books, tapes and videos abound in Christian bookstores about prosperity and riches. Television ministries have parishioners rushing to the alter, not to seek

---

[10] Baker, Jim. *Prosperity and the Coming Apocalypse*, Nashville, Tenn: Thomas Nelson Publishers, 1998. 27.

repentance, but to lay their bills or money at the feet of ministers who walk over the mammon to bless it. I even heard one televangelist advise that if the computers have Y2K glitches and their bills have been lost, Christians should not let their creditors know that they still owe the bill. He reasoned that this would be God's way of debt cancellation. The Bible would not call this debt cancellation because it is something else ...stealing.

The effect of the Church providing a moral underpinning to sins of the flesh has devastating effects. For instance, history reveals that the Church at one time provided a moral foundation to the sinful institution of slavery. The lasting effect of the Church's approval of slavery has been devastating on the world and the body of Christ. Comparatively, the scourge of materialism is one of Satan's last ditch attempts to steal the focus of the bride of Christ from the soon to arrive Bridegroom. It is a preparation for the deception of the beast power, when the choice will the ability to buy and/or sale, or to be in Gods will through sacrifice by refusing to align with the power of the Antichrist.

Now, at a time when the world is on the threshold of unspeakable tribulation and time of trouble and strife, the Church, God's Bastille of truth in a sin-sick world, has its focus on the material wealth of this world. I am deeply concerned that the majority of modern Christians are not preparing themselves spiritually for difficulties. This is the reason that I feel led to present this message of adversity.

Most importantly, the dominant presumptions have ill equipped many believers from the growth that can occur during difficult times. For instance, many of the wealthy who built their hopes on the material riches of this world during the early part of the twentieth century took their own lives when the market crashed. They were not prepared for the crisis through their relationship with Christ. Many Christians are now pinning their hopes on materialism that is causing an even more devastating spiritual death.

This is in no way to suggest that God will not bless us in all ways, including materially, and we have the assurance that when we pray, our prayers are heard. But, as servants of the Most High, we are to always pray that God's will be done. The current prosperity teaching is leading to ungodly excess and wrongful motivations within the Christian community and the church is being identified with this material excess. Conversely, Christians are to be known by our moderation. We are not to focus on material wealth, although we are to work hard and be good stewards of the wealth of which we are entrusted.

We are to always believe that God will take care of us, and we have been given the authority to approach God for all of the desires of our hearts. Our desires must always be ordered after Godliness. When we pray we should always be mindful of Paul's counsel on how God answers our petitions:

> Let your moderation be known unto all men. The lord is at hand.
> Be careful for nothing: but in every thing by prayer and supplication with thanksgiving let your requests be made known unto to God. And the peace of God, which passeth all understanding, shall keep your hearts and minds through Christ Jesus. (Phil. 4:5-7)

Rather than claiming material excess, we are instructed to be known by our moderation. When we have a need we are to make our petition known unto God and He will answer our prayers. Rather than demanding that God deliver to us what we want, when we want it, we are to make our petitions known in faith, and then we are to accept His answer to our plea. When we pray, we have not been promised our material wants, but rather the peace of God. This peace, which passes all understanding, will allow us to accept God's working in our lives. Our answer will be according to the Master's good will for our lives, and whether we are faced with abundance or lack, this peace will allow us to experience God working His perfect will in our lives.

While the modern prosperity teaching has many Christians focusing on material things, Paul goes on to teach us what should be our true focus:

> Finally brethren, whatsoever things are true, whatsoever things are honest, whatsoever things are just, whatsoever things are pure, whatsoever things are lovely, whatsoever things are of a good report; If there be any virtue, and if there be any praise, think on these things. (Phil.4:8)

BITTER OR BETTER: THE ADVERSITY PRINCIPLES

We are to focus on things which are honest, just, pure, lovely and of a good report; those things which have virtue and praise. Paul had a clear understanding of the balance that the adversity principle brings to the life of a Christian. By his knowledge of the adversity principle, Paul knew how to serve and praise God in whatever circumstance God placed him in and thus reflected the Sixth Principle of Adversity: *God allows adversity to give Christians the proper perspective of this world and the world to Come.*

PRINCIPLE VII: GOD ALLOWS ADVERSITY BECAUSE CHRISTIANS ARE SOLDIERS IN A GREAT CONFLICT BETWEEN GOOD AND EVIL

CHAPTER 11
HOW CHRISTIANS SHOULD RESPOND TO ADVERSITY

"Beloved, think it not strange concerning the fiery trials which is to try you, as though some strange thing happened unto you." I Peter 4:12

We have seen how God allowed adversity to help confront and heal the innermost spiritual problems of these giants in Biblical history. The question remains, how then should we as Christians respond to adversity in our lives?

We must first understand that we are involved in a war that is greater than our individual skirmishes with the adversary. As Christians we are soldiers in a great conflict that is waging between Christ and Satan. Although the outcome has already been settled, Christians are to continue to wage the war for the hearts and minds of men and women until Christ returns. As we deal with the adversity that enters our lives we must keep the Adversity Principle Number 7 in mind: *God allows adversity because Christians are soldiers in a great conflict between good and evil.*

First, it is very important to be reasonable and rational in our approach to dealing with adversity. We should not in any way condone or be prone to fanaticism. We should not invite adversity or put ourselves in a position to be faced with adverse situations. God gives us only good gifts but we have an adversary, Satan, who seeks to devour us at all times. While Satan seeks to accuse us and bring hardship into our lives, it is God who bends Satan's darts and uses them to allow "the called" to confront the issues of their hearts. Satan only has legal ground in our hearts in those places where sin resides, whether the sin is known or is hidden. When our sins are hidden, God allows the place that Satan has in us to expose our sin to us. Once the sin is exposed, we have the opportunity to approach God's throne for forgiveness, mercy and healing.

Remember, the battle is not yours, it's the Lords. Importantly, every time we have a small problem or stub our toe we should not try to figure out how God is using the adversity principle. Nevertheless, we should ever be open to God's leading in all of the circumstances of our lives. We should maintain a heightened awareness when circumstances are particularly difficult or when the same malady or situation continually occurs.

Before we examine our adversity experience under these principles, we should first consider whether we are being confronted with some other Biblical principle or admonition, such as sowing and reaping. Sowing and reaping, for example, is related to open and acknowledged sin. When we openly sin there are apparent consequences, even after we receive forgiveness for the sin. The Bible teaches us that we reap what we sow and, if we sow bad seeds, then we will reap the results of the sowing. Consequently, if we sow good seeds, we will also receive the results of this positive sowing. While many times it is difficult to see the direct correspondence of our actions, the Bible assures us of this correlation between our sowing actions and the life reaping results.

Importantly, if our adverse condition is as a result of open and acknowledged sin, the adversity principle is probably not being invoked. Since the principles of God are never in competition with one another, there are different spiritual strategies for dealing with God's working in our lives. For instance, if we find ourselves suffering from the result of our open violations of God's will, then we must know that when we come to forgiveness through Christ there are many avenues in which He will assist us through the difficulty. God has a way of even mitigating the results of the consequences of our sowing and reaping when we come to Him in repentance. God has not dealt with us "after our sins; nor rewarded us according to our iniquities,"(See Psalms 103:13). Since Christ is our sin bearer we don't have to suffer the full consequence of our sins.

Our response to the adversity principle is similar in some ways to the response for known sin, but it involves a heightened level of spiritual discernment. At the first sign of adversity the Christian should confess all known sin. This is a time when we must be very careful to tarry near the throne room of God. When adversity becomes manifest, Satan would have us close off our relationship with God in bitterness. We must consider that the same Holy One who numbers the hairs of our head and takes note of the sparrow that falls, is intimately involved with all of the circumstances of our lives.

It is crucial to remember from the outset that adversity does not mean that we are disfavored of God. When Satan whispers that we are being forsaken, call that rascal a liar and tread him under your feet. While the adversity may continue and, in fact, may intensify, the child of God must hold on and keep holding onto God's steady and unchanging hand. It may seem that during these times of adversity that God is being silent in your life but be not deceived, God is with you even when it does not feel like you are in His presence.

One of the deceptions that Satan has perpetrated on the body of Christ is the thought that to serve God means that we will have few real problems. Part of the dangers of the perverted prosperity and self-love presumptions is that they do not adequately prepare its adherents for the adversity that will surely come our way as Christians. Adversity may come into a Christian's life through a myriad of ways, such as family problems, financial pressures, interpersonal relationship concerns or even direct spiritual attack. However, the problems are not indicative of the whole story and it is important not to allow your feelings or present condition to deceive you. It is not about how you feel or even what you have materially that determines your destiny, it is a matter of knowing God and seeking His will that provides you with strength and solutions when adversity arrives.

Once we have confessed all known sin, we should then go into a period of intensive prayer and heart searching. It may be a good time to enter not only into prayer but also into fasting. Our aim and plea should be to ask God: "What would you have me do?" "Where would you have me go?" "Whom do you want me to serve?" Pay close attention to the area of your adversity, and ask yourself: "Have I experienced this type of adversity before"? Be open to whether God could be trying to reveal something specific to your experience with Him. Always remember in the midst of adversity to keep praising God for His goodness, mercy and grace.

During times of adversity, it is very important to listen for God's individual leading but His voice must always be verified and validated by the Scriptures. The study of God's word becomes even more important during these times. While it is important to study Bible passages that provide comfort, it is also important to be open to passages that offer correction. Allow God to bring to your consciousness those events in your life that may need to be resolved, particularly those family issues that you may have stuffed into the recesses of your mind. Be open to biblically based Christian counseling.

The reason I emphasize biblically based Christian counseling is that like Job, you may receive an abundance of opinions from associates and friends regarding the reasons for the adversity. Like Job, we must know what information to accept and what opinions to ignore. The Bible and the leading of the Holy Spirit must be the final arbiters of the counsel that you accept. Be particularly open to God's still small voice and allow Him to speak to your innermost heart. Again, and this cannot be stressed enough, validate all information through the filter of Scripture. It is crucial to remember that Satan endeavors to confuse you into thinking that God is not with you because of the adversity.

This is a time when your faith must be strengthened even though you may not feel God's presence. Reflect on how God allowed adversity in the lives of his most loved disciples. Consider how Job, Joseph, Moses and Paul, as well as others through the ages must have felt during their time of adversity. Their human emotions must have often been at odds with the faith that God was inspiring in their lives, but they did not allow their emotions to control the situation. The lesson is that while we should not ignore our emotions, they must not control us. When we ignore our emotions we are apt to enter into dysfunctional substitutes such as denial.

Embrace and consider your feelings because God has given us these emotions for a reason. Emotions must not control us, but they can help us deal with the situations of our lives. If you need to cry, cry and know that it is perfectly permissible with God. Be real. You may not need to cry a whimper; you may need to cry a storm. If you feel the need to verbalize to God your feelings, do that as well. This is the time to be absolutely open and honest with God. Do not withhold any thing that is going on with you in your conscious relationship with God. Consider that Paul's "thorn in the flesh" was never resolved, but God gave him the peace necessary to accept the situation. Whatever you do, do not allow bitterness to overtake you, remember God is endeavoring to make you better. Rejoice in the Lord always and again I say rejoice.

Importantly, reflect on how Christ overcame adversity. Accept with all your heart that God will strengthen you with the same power that facilitated Christ's ability to overcome. Contemplate on how Christ, at Gethsemane, when confronted with the choice of doing the will of the Father verses the immediate need of the flesh, chose the Father's perfect will for His life and so should we.

The Christian revelation of Christ is that while he was fully God He was also fully man. Even though He had the direct power of the universe immediately available to Him, Christ used no advantage to extricate Himself from adversity that is not immediately available to the Christian. In Gethsemane, Christ was so challenged by the adversity of the impending cross that his sweat was mingled with blood. The fact that He was sweating in the first place is indicative of Christ's human response to stress. The added information that His sweat was mingled with blood points to the extreme degree of His turmoil. This means that when Christ was faced with adversity, He faced it as a man but even more so than we do.

Whenever Satan challenged Christ, the enemy was completely defeated. Christ did not succumb to the temptation to sin and he was tempted at every point of human experience. Since Christ did not sin, He faced the full fury of Satan's temptation on every point. The only difference was that since Christ had never sinned, there was no legal ground in Christ himself for Satan to claim. Importantly, since Christ's ministry was substitutionary, one where his sinless life was lived so that we might have access to eternal life, Satan had the legal authority to tempt Christ in every area for which he was to be our substitute. Hence, the Bible says that Christ "was in all points tempted as we are, yet without sin,"(Romans 4:15).

We must also consider that Satan also had the full legal ground to challenge Christ when he hung on the cross, as He took our sin upon himself for the collective sin of the whole world. Imagine, the sinless Son of God was tempted with all of the discouragement and doubt that Satan could muster at a time when all external circumstances would indicate that Satan had won the great controversy. While Christ was suffering, the defeat seemed imminent but the suffering was just part of the success story. He seemed defeated while he was in the process of defeating the enemy for our sakes.

When faced with adversity we should never be discouraged with the extrinsic (outward) circumstances, but in the midst of trouble we should ever claim the promises of God. Things are not what they seem so do not ever allow discouragement to affect your decisions. Always claim the merits and power of Christ for your circumstances. Focus on the goodness of God through Christ while allowing the true condition of your heart to be exposed.

This should also be a time of particular honesty with God as you allow yourself to be examined and led by the only One who sees and knows all. While going through the crisis remember that you are unique to the God who created you and redeemed you. While you may gain strength from others who have gone through adversity, your uniqueness means that God is working for your good in a way that has been developed just for you.

Throughout the adversity, admit and confess any sin that is revealed. I assure you that if you refuse to allow yourself to become bitter, God will make you better through this experience. Even when it seems overwhelming, allow your faith to grow and remember how God has sustained you and others in the past. Praise God from whom all blessing flows and you will be blessed and made better through adversity.

Times of adversity also provide an important opportunity for the Church, the household of faith, to respond to the individual problems of its members. Unfortunately, many churches have bought so deeply into false presumptions that they do not provide a place of fellowship and comfort to those who are being challenged by adversity. Instead of being the haven of peace, repose, community support and strength that Christ intended the Church to be, these perverted doctrines cause Many Churches to castigate those whom are under challenge. The local Church congregation has an important role in assisting members through adversity.

One of the dangers of false presumptions in the church is that it keeps the household of faith from being the God-ordained bastion of comfort and support for its members who are facing adversity. Now that we have discussed how a Christian who is facing adversity should respond lets now consider the role of the Church in dealing with the adversity of its members.

CHAPTER 12
THE CHURCH AND THE ADVERSITY OF HER MEMBERS

"Beloved, think it not strange concerning the fiery trials which is to try you, as though some strange thing happened unto you." I Peter 4:12

The living God has given His Church power that is almost inconceivable. Imagine, Christ Himself instructed the Church that those things that we "bind on earth will be bound in heaven and those things that we loose on earth will be loosed in heaven" (See Matt. 18:18). Thus, the church is given power to be involved in the adversity experience of its members. When Satan enters the life of a church member through adversity, the church should always be willing to exercise its gifts and intercession authority on behalf of the individual member. If the church does not exercise its power as granted by Christ, the adversity experience may needlessly intensify. We must not lose sight of the Seventh Principle of Adversity: *God allows adversity because Christians are soldiers in a great conflict between good and evil.*

The Church has a vital role to play in the adversity experiences of its members as well as mediating for the adversity that is in the world. The Church's ultimate responsibility is to be a conduit for God's will on earth, whatever the reason for the adversity or the eventual outcome.

Unfortunately, the Church has often allowed the enemy to attack her members without a proper rebuke. Satan exults when erroneous presumptions position the Church to almost sacrifice her members by failing to understand the principles of adversity and the intercessory actions necessary for the success of the individual member. There is an outcome difference when the Church corporately fights against the attack of the enemy through praise and prayer, which is, in effect, an exercise of the ability to bind and loose. An impressive example of the role of the Church in corporately fighting adversity is found in the twelfth chapter of Acts. I recommend a complete reading of Acts 12 to provide a proper foundation for the Church's ability to intercede in the adversity experience of its members.

In this amazing incident of the early Church, Satan used wicked King Herod as an instrument of destruction and persecution. Herod arrested James, the brother of John, and had him killed by the sword. The mode of the execution of James suggests that a civil authority that utilized a Roman method of punishment decreed his death. Had James been charged with blasphemy or heresy, the Sanhedrin would have sentenced him to death by stoning. James' execution meant that civil government power was being employed against the early Church. This was an application of the fact that we "wrestle not against flesh and blood, but against principalities, against rulers of the darkness of this world, against spiritual wickedness in high places"(Eph. 6:12).

Amazingly, we have no record of the church responding in any way to the adversity brought forth by Herod. I am not suggesting that the Church should have taken up arms because the "weapons of our warfare are not carnal, but mighty through God to the pulling down of strongholds" (See 2 Cor. 10). The Church should have resorted to spiritual warfare to defeat the persecution of the enemy. When the enemy sounds the battle cry, the Church is instructed to prepare for the battle by taking on "the whole amour of God, that ye (we) may be able to withstand in the evil day, and having done all to stand" (Eph. 6:13). The Church is not to submit to the adversity experience brought forth by the devil. When the Church is silent, the enemy is more apt to have his way and will intensify his attacks.

In this case the Bible reflects that when Herod (under the influence of the enemy) saw that his persecution of the Church pleased the Jews, he went on to further persecute the Church by also taking Peter into custody. Now we have a situation where a leader of the early Church, James, is executed. Now we have Peter, another leader who was also the primary voice of the early Church, taken into captivity. This was an important time for the fledgling Christian movement and I am sure many wondered whether the Church would become just another victim of the powerful and oppressive Roman system. Would the early Church become another sect who, after losing its founder (Christ) to religious/governmentally imposed execution by crucifixion, would now be scattered as its leaders were tracked down and massacred?

The answer was a definitive one as the Church rose to fulfill its position as God's vessel of authority and strength on this earth. Unlike the silence recorded at the taking and killing of James, the Bible reveals that when Peter was taken into custody, the Church put on its full spiritual armaments in preparation for the battle against the enemy.

How did the Church now prepare for battle? By having on the right spiritual clothing. The Bible teaches that in order to stand against the power of the enemy we must have our loins girt about with truth. We must have on the breastplate of righteousness, have our feet shod with the preparation of the gospel of peace, and raise the shield of faith that allows us to withstand the fiery darts of the wicked. Of course, we must first have on the helmet of salvation (Eph. 6: 14-16). The Church, properly clothed, is ready to go on offense against the onslaught of the enemy through the "sword of the Spirit, which is the word of God, praying always with all prayer and supplication in the Spirit, and watching there unto with all perseverance and supplication for all saints"(Eph. 6: 17-18).

The evidence that the Church had on the full armor of God was the prayer and supplication that the members entered into when it was discovered that Peter had been taken into custody. This time the unceasing prayers of the people of God were used in resistance to Herod's efforts. The proactive stance of the Church released the power of God to intervene in the situation and the tide changed completely.

When Herod sought to bring Peter for execution, God intervened in this adversity experience in a most miraculous way. On the night that Peter was brought forth he was sleeping between two soldiers and was bound with chains. Talk about having confidence in the midst of adversity. Peter was schedule to be executed the next morning yet he was so sure of his position with God that he was sleeping like a baby. Peter's sleeping indicated that he knew his life was in the Master's hand and not his captors.

Suddenly a light shone in the prison and an angel touched Peter on the side to waken him. Peter was told him to arise quickly. As Peter arose, his chains miraculously fell from him as he followed the angel to safety. When Peter came to the home of Mary, mother of John Mark, and the place where many of the Christians were gathered together to pray, Peter was left at the door knocking while the young Rhoda went to tell the collected group that Peter was out at the gate.

We can only imagine the scene of praise and rejoicing when the collected prayer group realized that their prayers were being answered while they were still in the process of presenting their petitions to the Lord. The Church had prevailed in the adversity of Peter by using the spiritual weapon of prayer to release the power of God and the Lord sent an angel to intervene in the adversity. I believe that the participation of the Church literally saved the life of the man of God.

We must not ignore the implications for the modern Church. When the Church of the Living God did nothing, the enemy had his way by inspiring Herod to kill James without a rebuff. But when God's people came together to fight the good fight of faith and arm themselves with the spiritual weapon of prayer, angels were commissioned from on high to fight the battle to release Peter from harms way. The Church has the keys to release God's power on the earth. When we do nothing to help one another during adversity, we miss the opportunity to harness the power of God. When we do not enter into spiritual warfare, we not only fail to participate in the individual solution of a member, we fail to be used as an instrument to release God's power on earth.

When adversity presents itself in the life of a member of God's Church, we have an opportunity, and more importantly, a sacred responsibility, to intervene on behalf of our brothers and sisters in Christ. The Church is designed to be more then just a place for the eleven o'clock praise and worship service, and is more than the gathering place for compassionate people to combine their resources for the care of the poor. The Church even has an even more important function than the organization that provides a moral foundation for society.

As important as these other functions may be, the most important role of the Church is to be a militant organization, ordained by God to exercise spiritual power. The Church is actually an instrument of war that God will use for the defeat of the enemy in the lives of its members, and to reveal His character of love to the world. All of the functions of the Church should be in preparation for the spiritual warfare that we are ordained to fight.

For instance, when we enter into our praise and worship service, we are actually in preparation for battle. We praise God for his lordship and majesty but we also praise him for the victory. Praise acknowledges God's goodness for the battles that He has fought for us and through us and for the victories to come. Through our testimony we praise the Lord for his past deliverance and care. Through the eye of faith we praise Him for the deliverance to come. Our praise and worship service is one way that we take up the battle flag.

When the Church wakes up to its role as the army of God on this earth, Satan and his minions will be put on the run. Instead of fighting each other, as Christians are prone to do, we will be fighting for the lives of our members against the onslaught on the enemy. "Remember them that are in bonds, as bound with them; and them which suffer adversity, as being yourselves also in the body" (Heb. 13:3). The writer of Hebrews leaves no doubt as to how we should respond to the adversity of others. When a person within our purview suffers adversity, the Christian should consider that adversity as if were our own. We are to particularly remember the conditions of our Church members so that we can participate in their adversity. This precept is in complete harmony with the golden rule. "Do unto others as you would have them do unto you."

The Church is designed to be a mighty army. Many times the enemy has our fellow warriors in bondage and we must participate in getting them out. Unfortunately, the Church often fails to organize itself as a fighting force but it is now time to reorganize. For instance, each local Church should be structured so that the membership at large knows what is going on with each member. This is not the meddling, busybody inquiring of nosey people, but a true heartfelt acknowledgment that we are all in this fight together.

To accomplish this structure, each church should consider having a subcategory or small group consisting of ten to twenty of the saints. Each member of the small group would have responsibility to be in touch with the other small group members on a consistent basis. The small group members would be intimately involved in the lives of the other members in the group. Importantly, each group would never exercise any political influence within the Church itself. The small groups would not be in competition with other groups or have any use other than to monitor, pray and share with other group members. The small groups would only exercise the admonition of Ephesians 6:18 that we should be "watching thereunto with all perseverance and supplication for all Saints."

Whenever a member of the group encounters any problems or challenges the other members of the group would be made aware and appropriate action would be taken. Most importantly, in special situations of extreme adversity the whole Church would be informed so that corporate action could be taken.

The utility of the small group modality is important because individual members have traditionally dealt with their adversity experience alone. The Church was designed by God to be more intimate, more involved and more proactive than any other organization on the face of the earth. Yet the modern Church member is often more distanced and estranged from fellow members than those they work with, go to school with or even those with whom they attend sporting events. The power of the church is limited by our failure to be intimately involved with each other's lives.

We have become accustomed to viewing the Church as the place where we go to worship or to attend a service (i.e., weddings, funerals etc.), rather then a place to lay down our burdens and pick up our spiritual weapons. The Church has many functions and we must have balance to proceed in the way that God would ordain. Yes, the Church is a hospital for sinners, but it is also a place to gather for power to overcome. The Church is a place to sing hymns and hear from God through sermons, but it is also a place to be equipped for spiritual warfare. Church is a place where we share our joys and sorrows but it is also a place where we find solutions for our problems. Most importantly, the Church is a place to share and learn solutions for all of our natural and spiritual situations. How God must grieve when he sees individual Church members going through difficulties alone when he has provided an organization on this earth so that we would never have to be alone.

The correct application of the Church is particularly important as we enter the closing scenes of earth's history. While there are awesome times of trouble ahead for this world, the Church member must know that the Church is the place of rest and repose. The Church has an important part to play in the adversity experiences of its member both now and in the thrilling times to come.

CHAPTER 13
APPLICATIONS OF THE ADVERSITY PRINCIPLES FOR THE LAST DAYS

"And the dragon was wroth with the woman, and went to make war with her seed, which keep the commandments of God, and have the testimony of Jesus Christ." Revelations 12:17

A review of Prophecy reveals that we are living in the last days. During the closing scenes of Earth's history, God is endeavoring to develop a people who will trust Him completely which will, in turn, enable them to stand against the final onslaught of Satan. This is a wonderful time to be alive as one of God's chosen. Like Job, we must develop a relationship with God that allows us, through faith, to know that we are in God's will and care even when all evidence of earthly support has departed. It is not community approval or outward success that will enable us to stand in these delusional last days. We will overcome by having a trusting relationship with the Father through Jesus Christ. We must ever remember the Adversity Principle Number 7: *God allows adversity because Christians are soldiers in a great conflict between good and evil.*

The war that we fight is the only conflict that is won through surrender. Surrender is a very important, but under discussed aspect of the Christian experience. When we think of surrender, it often brings the connotation of defeat or inactivity. Surrender, within the Christian context, is a very active, positive posture. Surrender to God's will does not mean to just put up with whatever situation we are in and lethargically do nothing. Surrender to God means to "let go and let God." We learn to yield to the direction that God is leading, while putting forth the maximum energy to lean the crucial lessons and proceed to the next exciting step.

Within this context, surrender is an action position that allows us to have the inner peace necessary to survive the negative of the moment, while always maintaining the outer energy necessary to be ready for God's next step in our lives. Surrender does not mean that we resign ourselves to difficult situations. Our surrender to God's purpose illustrates that we have graduated from doubt to the realization that God is in control. As God exercises His divine sovereignty, we are free to do our part in submission to His will.

Surrender is powerful not powerless. In fact, surrender allows us to be part of the Omnipotent power of the universe. When we surrender to God's will we place ourselves at the disposal of His Omnipotent power and absolutely nothing can defeat us. No matter how the difficult the experience seems, surrender allows us to recognize how God is with us and has provided a way of escape. When we surrender to the will of God, He will work out the present situation for and through us, in ways that are unimaginable. He does this for the simple reason that He is God and knows all of the intricacies of the situation. When we are surrendered, we allow the Master to work it out for us.

We must not allow Satan to deceive us into thinking that adversity means that we are not in God's will. Though we may seem to lose all that we have, we have the assurance from God that He is with us "until the end." This is crucial to know as we face times of unparalleled adversity and societal pressure. During the time of our adversity we have the example of Job to be assured that we have nothing to fear, even though we may seem to lose it all. By remembering Job's victory we can face the frontal attacks of the enemy and know that God is still sovereign and is working on our behalf. We must ever remember that our Redeemer lives and that he will stand in the latter day and it is He who will come to save us and no other.

As Joseph was gifted to serve his generation, God's people will be gifted in these last days to finish the work. But, as we can see from the example of Joseph, we must not be lifted up with pride as our gifting comes. It's time for the Church of God to stop bragging about having the truth and start exercising the truth in love. We need to immediately utilize all of our gifts for the uplifting of God's people and His kingdom and expect to be gifted in even more spectacular ways as the need arises. May we each submit ourselves and our gifts to God for His good pleasure and so that He may use us to touch the lives of the unsaved and assist His children to make it home.

The example of Moses should convince us that God can heal every issue of our heart. We must ever internalize the point that God can be trusted, even though the innermost issues of our hearts rise to make us fall short. We should also understand that God is working it out for our good and we will prevail, through His power, if we love Him and are called according to His purpose. In the interim, we must allow the adversity in our lives to reveal the true issues of our hearts. Like Moses, we must rest assured that God is using the adversity of the wilderness to equip us for the ministry to come. Further, we must submit ourselves to ensure that every point of sin and dysfunction is given fully to the Master.

The adversity principles are used by God to assist the Christian pilgrim as we make our way in this sin sick world. When Christ returns, this and other stratagem that the Master put in place to help us through the sin environment will be no more. In fact, when Christ establishes His perfect kingdom, faith will be sight and the mysteries will be revealed because "now we see through a glass darkly, but then face to face: now I know it part; but then I shall know even as I am known"(I Cor. 13: 12).

Just before Christ's return, Satan's penchant for deception will increase as he takes a twofold approach. First, he will advance his efforts to mislead the world as he intensifies his persecution of God's children. It will seem as though the true followers of God have been abandoned because this persecution is directed toward "the called." When the irreverent observe the persecution of the righteous, they will use this situation to mock God's protection. If we are not careful to preserve the integrity of God's word, the erroneous modern presumptions that have infiltrated the Church will be used against us.

The potential for God to be mocked by the sinful world during this time is enhanced if the Church continues to embrace false doctrines. The unregenerate will point to erroneous teachings such as the perverted prosperity and self-love movement and ridicule the supposed failure of God to protect against adversity. We must be ever careful to cry aloud God's true message to this last generation in the present environment of peace, so that when these ever more perilous times arrive upon the Earth, we will have witnessed to this inevitability.

Second, Satan endeavors to deceive the Church. He hopes that when his persecutions are allowed to intensify, God's people will not have the necessary knowledge base and relationship with Him and each other to stand at a time of great pressure and persecution. Our hope is based upon our relationship with the Lord, and that relationship must be based upon the truth of His word. During this time of trouble, we will either be forced to a position of total trust that transcends the outward circumstance, or we will descend to a position of disillusionment. The enemy's plan is to deceive Christians into operating from wrong premises before the persecutions and temptations arise so that when tested we will be prone to discouragement. Our outcome, and the world's ability to see the example of Godliness that will lead to repentance, will depend upon our being in right relationship with the principles of God.

It is therefore extremely important that we allow truth to immediately root out these perverted, modern presumptions from the Church. The time is now because we are on the precipice of this crushing time of adversity. If the Church is operating out of wrong underlying principles when the time of adversity comes, many within the body of Christ will be deceived and will fail to properly represent our Creator and Redeemer. The reason that Paul was so emphatic about preserving the integrity of the gospel message was so that we, the Church, can be the salt and light that is needed during the dark days of the world.

Salt is used in little doses to change the flavor of the whole dish to which it is added. It is also used to purify and preserve foods to which it is added. Additionally, light, no matter how small, will completely change the darkness that it encounters. It is imperative for the world to see the Church reflecting the foundational truths of the gospel as we reject any movement that embraces false presumptions. As God prepares us for these last days, the church must be the salt and light necessary to fight the enemy on his territory.

There is nothing to fear. In fact, as we see perilous times approaching, we should be in great anticipation to be used by God in special ways. The patriarchs and prophets, as well as disciples throughout the ages, desired to be in this last day generation. We should be honored, not to be taken out of adversity, but to be a part of the generation that God will use through adversity in a mighty way. Are you prepared to be a salt in the midst of spoilage and light in the midst of darkness?

Right now, we should be celebrating His goodness and mercy, His protection and grace. In this time of peace and prosperity, we should be shouting before the King of Glory. This acknowledgment of praise to our Lord must continue regardless of the circumstances. If we begin our victory shout now, God will carry us through then.

As you reflect on the seven principles of adversity and examine and reexamine the encounters of God's chosen as they confronted their adversity experiences, try to remember these points:

1. Adversity comes to us in the form of trials, temptations and tests. Our reaction to the adversity either shows glory to God or areas of need for our further growth.

2. God does not cause adversity but He allows the attacks of the enemy, which occur on Satan's legal ground, to reveal to us our points of mistrust. The healing power of God, through His marvelous grace, will correct our revealed areas of faults and weaknesses as we surrender to His will.

3. During times of adversity we must learn to *talk our trust* and *not our fears* as we learn the lessons of God's trustworthiness and the need to surrender to His sovereign will.

4. Surrender does not mean defeat. Surrender is the submission of our will and the seeking of God's will regardless of the present circumstances.

5. We must learn to live in the moment because eternity is found in embracing God in the present circumstance, whatever they may be.

6. When faced with adversity we must never become bitter because of our present situation. Instead, we should embrace the sovereignty of God as we use the Biblical methods of response: Praise, prayer, meditation, fasting, confession, the study and claiming of God's word and the sharing of the word with others as we deal with the situation at hand.

7. Finally, if we do not become bitter when adversity confronts us,

we will be made better because of the experience.

What are the issues of your heart? Whether it is fear, pride or the deceitfulness that comes from the secrets of your childhood, God will expose and heal you if you will just grow through the adverse conditions of your life. Learn to embrace the adversity that our loving Creator has allowed into your life and be persuaded that you will become better from the experience.

It is God's will that we each endeavor to understand how His hand is curing the deepest problems of our heart. When adversity comes, do not allow Satan to make you bitter. Classify the adversity within one of the seven principles. Know that if we truly love God and are "the called" according to "His purpose", we can claim the promise that God is working to make us better. It is then that we can say, with assurance, that in our own experience all of the events of our lives, including the adversity, fall within the promise that "[a]ll things work together for good to them that love the Lord to them who are the called according to His purpose."

References and Sources

1. Baker, Jim. *I was Wrong.* Nashville, Tenn: Thomas Nelson, Inc. Publishers, 1996.

2. – – . *Prosperity and the Coming Apocalypse.* Nashville, Tenn: Thomas Nelson Publishers, 1998.

3. Bridges, Jerry. *The Discipline of Grace.* Colorado Springs, CO: Navpress, 1994.

4. Brownback, Paul. *The Danger of Self-Love.* Chicago: Moody Press, 1982.

5. Fudge, Edward. *The Fire That Consumes, A Biblical and Historical Study of Final Punishment.* Houston, Texas: Providential Press, 1982.

6. Kendall, R.T.. *God Meant it for Good: A Fresh Look at the Life of Joseph.* Morningstar Publications: Charlotte, NC, 1986.

7. Mazat, Don. *Christ-Esteem.* Eugene, Oregon: Harvest House 1990.

8. Pinnock, Clark. *The Destruction of the Finally Impenitent*, 1990.

9. Piper, John. "Is Self-Love Biblical?" Christianity Today, 12 August 1977, pp. 6-9, as quoted in Paul Brownback, *The Danger of Self-Love.* Chicago: Moody Press, 1982.

10. Stott, John. in the Anglican church and author of *Evangelical*

Essentials, 1988 pages 313-320.

11. **Wenham, John.** *The Goodness of God*, 1974; *Universalism and the Doctrine of Hell*, 1991; *The Case for Conditional Immortality.*

Selected Bible Texts on Adversity

Psalms 31:7, 8— I will be glad and rejoice in thy mercy: for thou hast considered my trouble; thou hast known my soul in adversities; And hast not shut me up into the hand of the enemy: thou hast set my feet in a large room.

Psalms 94:12-14— Blessed [is] the man whom thou chastenest, O LORD, and teachest him out of thy law; That thou mayest give him rest from the days of adversity, until the pit be digged for the wicked. For the LORD will not cast off his people, neither will he forsake his inheritance.

Prov. 17:17 — A friend loveth at all times, and a brother is born for adversity.

Prov. 24:10— [If] thou faint in the day of adversity, thy strength [is] small.

Eccle 7:14— In the day of prosperity be joyful, but in the day of adversity consider: God also hath set the one over against the other, to the end that man should find nothing after him.

Isaiah 30:20 — And [though] the Lord give you the bread of adversity, and the water of affliction, yet shall not thy teachers be removed into a corner any more, but thine eyes shall see thy teachers:

Hebrews 13:3— Remember them that are in bonds, as bound with them; [and] them which suffer adversity, as being yourselves also in the body.

Selected Bible Texts on Trials

Proverbs 17:3— The fining pot [is] for silver, and the furnace for gold: but the LORD trieth the hearts.

II Cor. 8:1-2— Moreover, brethren, we do you to wit of the grace of God bestowed on the churches of Macedonia how that in a great trial of affliction the abundance of their joy and their deep poverty abounded unto the riches of their liberality.

Hebrews 11:33:40 — Who through faith subdued kingdoms, wrought righteousness, obtained promises, stopped the mouths of lions, quenched the violence of fire, escaped the edge of the sword, out of weakness were made strong, waxed valiant in fight, turned to flight the armies of the aliens. Women received their dead raised to life again: and others were tortured, not accepting deliverance; that they might obtain a better resurrection. And others had trial of [cruel] mockings and scourgings, yea, moreover of bonds and imprisonment. They were stoned, they were sawn asunder, were tempted, were slain with the sword: they wandered about in sheepskins and goatskins; being destitute, afflicted, tormented, (Of whom the world was not worthy:) they wandered in deserts, and [in] mountains, and [in] dens and caves of the earth. And these all, having obtained a good report through faith, received not the promise. God, having provided some better thing for us, that they without us should not be made perfect.

Selected Bible Texts on Temptations

Psalms 95:8— Harden not your heart, as in the provocation, [and] as [in] the day of temptation in the wilderness.

Matthew 6:13— And lead us not into temptation, but deliver us from evil: For thine is the kingdom, and the power, and the glory, for ever. Amen.

Matthew 26:41— Watch and pray, that ye enter not into temptation: the spirit indeed [is] willing, but the flesh [is] weak.

Mark 14:38— Watch ye and pray, lest ye enter into temptation. The spirit truly [is] ready, but the flesh [is] weak.

Luke 4:13— And when the devil had ended all the temptation, he departed from him for a season.

Luke 8:11-13— Now the parable is this: The seed is the word of God. Those by the way side are they that hear; then cometh the devil, and taketh away the word out of their hearts, lest they should believe and be saved. They on the rock [are they], which, when they hear, receive the word with joy; and these have no root, which for a while believe, and in time of temptation fall away.

Luke 11:4— And forgive us our sins; for we also forgive every one that is indebted to us. And lead us not into temptation; but deliver us from evil.

Luke 22:40— And when he was at the place, he said unto them, Pray that ye enter not into temptation.

Luke 22:46— And said unto them, Why sleep ye? rise and pray, lest ye enter into temptation.

I Cor 10:13— There hath no temptation taken you but such as is common to man: but God [is] faithful, who will not suffer you to be tempted above that ye are able; but will with the temptation also make a way to escape, that ye may be able to bear [it]

Galations 4:13-14— Ye know how through infirmity of the flesh I preached the gospel unto you at the first. And my temptation which was in my flesh ye despised not, nor rejected; but received me as an angel of God, [even] as Christ Jesus.

I Tim. 6:9-11— But they that will be rich fall into temptation and a snare, and [into] many foolish and hurtful lusts, which drown men in destruction and perdition. For the love of money is the root of all evil: which while some coveted after, they have erred from the faith, and pierced themselves through with many sorrows. But thou, O man of God, flee these things; and follow after righteousness, godliness, faith, love, patience, meekness.

Hebrews 3:8— Harden not your hearts, as in the provocation, in the day of temptation in the wilderness:

James 1:12:15— Blessed [is] the man that endureth temptation: for when he is tried, he shall receive the crown of life, which the Lord hath promised to them that love him. Let no man say when he is tempted, I am tempted of God: for God cannot be tempted with evil, neither tempteth he any man. But every man is tempted, when he is drawn away of his own lust, and enticed. Then when lust hath conceived, it bringeth forth sin: and sin, when it is finished, bringeth forth death.

I Peter 1:6-7— Wherein ye greatly rejoice, though now for a season, if need be, ye are in heaviness through manifold temptations: That the trial of your faith, being much more precious than of gold that perisheth, though it be tried with fire, might be found unto praise and honour and glory at the appearing of Jesus Christ.

I Peter4:12-19— Beloved, think it not strange concerning the fiery trial which is to try you, as though some strange thing happened unto you: But rejoice, inasmuch as ye are partakers of Christ's sufferings; that, when his glory shall be revealed, ye may be glad also with exceeding joy.

If ye be reproached for the name of Christ, happy [are ye]; for the spirit of glory and of God resteth upon you: on their part he is evil spoken of, but on your part he is glorified. But let none of you suffer as a murderer, or [as] a thief, or [as] an evildoer, or as a busybody in other men's matters. Yet if [any man suffer] as a Christian, let him not be ashamed; but let him glorify God on this behalf. For the time [is come] that judgment must begin at the house of God: and if [it] first [begin] at us, what shall the end [be] of them that obey not the gospel of God? And if the righteous scarcely be saved, where shall the ungodly and the sinner appear? Wherefore let them that suffer according to the will of God commit the keeping of their souls [to him] in well doing, as unto a faithful Creator.

Acts 20:19— Serving the Lord with all humility of mind, and with many tears, and temptations, which befell me by the lying in wait of the Jews.

James 1:2-4— My brethren, count it all joy when ye fall into divers temptations; Knowing [this], that the trying of your faith worketh patience. But let patience have [her] perfect work, that ye may be perfect and entire, wanting nothing.

I Peter 1:6-7— Wherein ye greatly rejoice, though now for a season, if need be, ye are in heaviness through manifold temptations. That the trial of your faith, being much more precious than of gold that perisheth, though it be tried with fire, might be found unto praise and honour and glory at the appearing of Jesus Christ.

II Peter 2:9— The Lord knoweth how to deliver the godly out of temptations, and to reserve the unjust unto the day of judgment to be punished.

Rev. 3:10— Because thou hast kept the word of my patience, I also will keep thee from the hour of temptation, which shall come upon all the world, to try them that dwell upon the earth.

Printed in the United States
17632LVS00002B/1-51